# Philosophical Problems of the Social Sciences

*David Braybrooke*

DALHOUSIE UNIVERSITY

## Sources in Philosophy

A MACMILLAN SERIES
*Lewis White Beck, General Editor*
THE MACMILLAN COMPANY, NEW YORK
COLLIER–MACMILLAN LIMITED, LONDON

*Third Printing, 1966*

Library of Congress catalog card number 65-11066

THE MACMILLAN COMPANY, NEW YORK

COLLIER-MACMILLAN CANADA, LTD., TORONTO, ONTARIO

*Printed in the United States of America*

I wish to thank Professors Alexander D. MacDonald and Herbert A. Simon for their friendly aid and advice in connection with the selection on mathematical constructions; Professor Lewis W. Beck, the general editor of the series in which this book is to appear, for his perceptive and tactful general editing; Phyllis Knox and David K. House for help in preparing the manuscript; my wife Alice for joining me in proofreading; and the students of my P. P. E. seminar at Dalhousie during 1963–64 for cheerfully submitting to a trial run of the argument mounted in my introduction. The Dalhousie University Research and Development Fund for the Humanities and the Social Sciences paid for certain connected expenses.

D.B.

*Halifax*

# Contents

# Introduction

## I. PHILOSOPHICAL SORTING

One of the chief things that philosophy encourages people to do is to sort out questions: *a priori* questions from empirical questions, for instance; and moral questions from neutral questions of fact. This sorting is itself a human activity, with purposes of its own, governed by its own distinctive concepts of success or failure. It is directed at illuminating other human activities, including other activities of inquiry. Engaged in those activities, men ask questions about mathematical relationships; about events in nature; about actions in society. Engaged in philosophy, men ask questions about questions: What sorts of concepts generate the questions raised in different activities of inquiry? What procedures of investigation, what kinds of answers, do those questions imply? Philosophy seeks to understand the activities in which the questions figure by understanding the sorts of concepts that figure in the questions.

The chief thing that this book aims to do is to furnish the reader with a philosophical principle of sorting that is peculiarly applicable to questions in the social sciences. This principle distinguishes between questions about human *behavior* and questions about human *action;* and, correspondingly, between two different activities of inquiry and two different kinds of explanation. The relevance of this principle is a leading point of difference between social science and natural science respecting conceptions of inquiry; and the principle is a leading factor in determining how far philosophical findings respecting the natural sciences carry over into philosophical findings respecting the social ones. The principle also helps to identify the complications caused in social science by the mutual impact of "values" and "facts"; for the impact is different—more intimate and more troublesome—in the case of action questions.

The terms "behavior" and "action" are not self-explanatory. They are not even entirely suitable, since even in this book they are sometimes used interchangeably. One has to learn how to use them in a special way, along with learning how to use the special distinction embodied in the behavior-action principle of sorting. Reflecting on the materials collected in this book, the reader will begin to use the principle to do some sorting of his own. He will begin to appreciate

1

some of the subtleties of using it. He will be able to carry it away, substantially understood and partly tested, to illuminate further studies in social science.

He will also be able to carry it away to illuminate further studies in philosophy. The philosophical analysis of *ethics* invites coordination with philosophical findings about social science, since social science describes and explains the same human activities which ethics appraises and seeks to direct. Moreover, it will turn out that the central and recurrent preoccupations of philosophy with the analysis of language and meaning fit into the action branch of the social sciences. In every direction, doing philosophy (well or badly) is—for better or for worse—one way of doing social science.

## II. THE BEHAVIOR–ACTION DISTINCTION

A great deal of the work done by social scientists consists in collecting facts to answer particular questions. Sometimes these questions are posed in ordinary language: In what (else) do people who support freedom of speech differ from people who do not? Are the people who obtain power by and large the same people who most desire it? Sometimes the questions are posed in terms introduced by social scientists: Is the tax structure of Nova Scotia regressive? Has mobility into the business elite increased or decreased? Precise and well-founded answers to such questions are not easy to come by. They can generally be obtained only by expert clarification of terms and by judiciously directed statistical investigations—in other words, by activities which by themselves vindicate the dignity of specialized social science.

However, social scientists undertake to do a good deal more than collect facts expertly. They commonly try to work up more or less elaborate *explanations* of their findings. They try to explain why some exercises of power are regarded as legitimate, and others illegitimate; how it happens that regressive taxes survive in countries with majoritarian governments; what factors count for most in increasing or decreasing vertical mobility; how people come to differ in their conceptions of free speech.

The behavior-action principle of sorting arises in the midst of conflicting philosophical pronouncements about the character of such explanations.

According to some pronouncements, when naïve objections to

scientific investigation of human affairs have been disposed of—by arguments like those advanced by Skinner (in the first selection below, p. 19)—the social sciences may proceed with the same methods as the natural sciences, in the expectation of discovering the same sort of explanations. Popper (see p. 32) characterizes this unity of method by emphasizing very general features of theory-construction: social scientists, like natural scientists, formulate hypotheses; deduce testable consequences; eliminate hypotheses whose consequences do not withstand testing. Thus they arrive at empirical laws about the connections of phenomena.

Skinner (in the second selection from him, beginning p. 42) expresses the natural-scientific orientation in a more particularized form. He offers to explain how, item by item, organisms evolve repertoires of behavior. An organism will repeat items that are reinforced (favored) [1] by the environment; it will discard items that fail to be reinforced (or happen to be reinforced negatively). The frequency with which a given item appears depends upon the frequency with which it has been reinforced, and upon other quantifiable variables—variables associated, for instance, with the physical state of the organism, and with the degree to which situations now occurring resemble past situations in which reinforcements were forthcoming. By identifying and observing such variables, Skinner proposes to give quantitative treatment to what may be called *the elementary subject matter of the social sciences:* the actions and behavior of individual persons.

It is just this elementary subject matter, however, which most sharply poses the problem of suitable explanation. Where Skinner, treating persons as organisms, would undertake to show how the probability of a person's behaving one way or another in a given situation depends on the amount and timing of previous conditioning, other writers like Schutz (see p. 53) and Moore and Anderson (see p. 68) call for explanations apparently wholly different in conception.

These writers concern themselves primarily not with counting or measuring reinforcements and responses, but with discovering the *meaning* of actions. Schutz would ask of a given action, how am I to understand it?—which is to ask, in the first place, what would a person doing it conceive it to be? and, in the second place, what (given this conception of it) are the motives and reasons that any-

[1] For Skinner's definition of reinforcement, see p. 48 below.

one might have for doing it? To explain, with these questions in mind, what an action is and why it is done requires attention simultaneously to the socially-formed personalities of the people who might do such an action and to the social contexts in which they might do it.

The concepts that figure in an action—which an action exemplifies because the person who does it means it to be an action so conceived—are typically concepts that are shared and learned socially. Their applications in shaping actions, like their manifestations in language, are governed by social rules, or norms (indeed, speech-acts are on this view just a special case of actions generally). To act meaningfully in a given society is to act—for good or ill—according to the norms, or rules, that define the kinds of possible actions by defining the criteria for assigning actions to one kind rather than another. Moreover, it is by acting in such a context of rules and incorporating rules into their own conduct that people develop specifically human personalities and characters.[2]

Which is the right approach to explanation? If a determined attempt were made to sort out all the questions in the elementary subject matter of social science that called for "action" explanations, would there be any left to be dealt with by "behavior" explanations? If a determined effort were made to carry through Skinner's program, would action explanations become superfluous?

The answer that seems to make most sense of the conflicting assertions displayed in this book is that some questions, investigations, and explanations clearly belong on the action side and some—just as clearly—on the behavior side, while others, equally important in social science, cannot readily and unambiguously be assigned to either.

## III. TWO KINDS OF QUESTIONS

Both action questions and behavior questions can be raised about the same social phenomenon. Let us consider, as an example of something that might occur within the elementary subject matter, a man handing an assortment of small gold discs to another man.[3]

[2] Cf., with Schutz (at p. 61 below) and Moore and Anderson, Aristotle, *Nicomachean Ethics*, Bk. II, Chaps. 1–2.

[3] Cf. the examples cited from Max Weber by Peter Winch, in *The Idea of a Social Science and Its Relation to Philosophy* (London: Routledge & Kegan Paul Ltd., 1958), p. 117.

Why is he doing it? He might be handing them *on* for the next stage in engraving; or handing them *back* for further polishing. Are they medals, being prepared for awarding? If they were coins, he might be lending a month's rent to a friend; or depositing money in a bank; donating his life's savings to a retired seamen's home; or offering his choicest coins for display at a numismatic exhibition.

Clearly, these are all different actions, meant to fulfill different criteria; and in their turn they elicit different actions from other people. The parties to such interactions would understand, for example, that the criteria which acts of lending must meet differ from the criteria for acts of giving. The same norms that supply the criteria for participants would, moreover, supply them for observers. Observers seeking to classify the actions as falling under one set of concepts rather than another would take into account differences envisaged in the norms, or rules, of the social context—differences in the forms of words used, differences in expectations, differences in temporal and physical setting.

So far the example tells wholly on the action side; and the action side can make much more of it. Actions vary in richness or poverty of meaning. To hand something over is a different action from letting it drop (when, by chance, someone is present to catch it). Both actions, however, are alike in being relatively poor in conceptual connections, a fact that makes it possible for them to figure as ingredients in any of a multitude of more complex actions. By contrast, the action of offering some prized coins for exhibition by a numismatic society is richly clothed with concepts and norms, many of them unheard-of in other cultures.

It might seem that people know all about the concepts and norms associated with actions in their own culture. But this is not true. There are likely to be all sorts of activities into which they have not been fully initiated even as adults. Furthermore, they have often not formulated the criteria which they employ in making their own actions distinct. People learn to act, as they learn to speak, very largely by imitation; or by heeding corrections that impose social norms without formulating them. Indeed, besides making explicit conventions that have hitherto been followed implicitly, setting forth the concepts and norms embodied in actions may bring to light conventions whose content may not have been suspected by the people acting in accordance with them.

Further inquiries introduce themselves at this stage. Are there not families of actions—and of typical action-situations—which embody whole systems of norms or rules? Religious activities would seem to form one such family; economic activities, another. The variety of actions falling into either family differs from culture to culture and from one period of history to another. The people who take part in the activities can no more be expected than outsiders to characterize such differences without reflection and research. (Indeed, victims of ideological nearsightedness, they may have to reflect harder than outsiders.) Finally, there are discoveries to be made about the characteristics of cultures as wholes: for instance, the characterization of Western civilization as strenuously and cumulatively rational, which we owe immediately to Max Weber, and perhaps ultimately to the philosopher Hegel (from whom Marx learned much the same lesson).

Does the example about the man handing over the gold discs then belong entirely to the action side? Is there no room for behavior explanations, to be sought by natural-scientific methods like Skinner's?

Suppose it is agreed that *what* the man is doing is not only handing over some gold discs, but (a richer description) handing them *back* for further polishing. There are behavior questions to ask and answer about this action or phenomenon.

The action involves a procedure for inspection; rejection; and renewing someone else's task. May it not be asked, in the first place, how the man performing the action acquired this procedure? In reply, it would be relevant to explain how behavior in accordance with the procedure had been reinforced, while behavior divergent from it had not been. For instance, when the man first came on the job, the foreman stood beside him, nodding his head when some discs were passed on or passed back, intervening at other times to redirect the discs. Is this process of conditioning essentially different from the process by which *pigeons* acquire procedures of industrial inspection? [4]

The procedure for inspecting gold discs does not stand alone in the subject's behavior. It belongs to an extensive repertoire of procedures for various actions—all the many actions which the subject

[4] See the pictures on p. 24 of Clifford T. Morgan, *Introduction to Psychology* (2d ed.; New York: McGraw-Hill Book Co., Inc., 1961) which show a pigeon watching a passing conveyor belt for badly painted parts, pecking at his window when he sees one.

has learned to do. One may therefore ask, in the second place, how was the repertoire acquired? How is it maintained? These, too, are questions on the behavior side. They are suitably answered by citing the reinforcements, strong or weak, that the subject receives, and on what schedules—regular or variable; continuous or intermittent—the environment provides them; and by indicating which sorts of schedules operate most quickly to establish items in a repertoire, which most lastingly.

Action questions about personal conduct lead immediately, as we have seen, to questions about interaction and shared concepts; they then expand into questions about families of actions and into attempts at characterizing the general context of rules, or norms—the whole culture—within which these families subsist. Behavior questions about the same elementary subject matter are likewise susceptible of expansion. They, too, lead to questions about interaction (e.g., with the foreman); and eventually to attempts at explaining the origin and survival of particular institutions, presuming that successful institutions have the features which they do because those features are functionally adapted to the necessities and opportunities of the environment.

The system of norms constituting the factory organization in which the disc inspector, the foreman, and the polishers interact in their distinct ways evolved from earlier institutional forms. It reflects the reinforcements provided by the environment in the past; it survives because of a continuing schedule of reinforcements in the present—mutual support and satisfaction on the factory floor; profits rather than losses in the front office. It rests upon quantitative relations affecting interaction like those treated by Simon in his discussion of group equilibrium (p. 94 ff. below).

The expansion of behavior questions need not stop with particular institutions. The same sort of questions may be asked about whole societies. Some societies survive, because their distinctive institutions are adapted to the environment; others disintegrate, because the policies put forward by their institutions fail to be reinforced. The evolutionary scheme of explanation that behavior questions are designed to elicit thus has a part to play in the most ambitious regions of history and political science.

The result, then, of applying the behavior-action principle to the elementary subject matter of social science and to questions—opening out of that subject matter—about its immediate and less immediate contexts is to sort out questions on both the behavior and the action sides.

## IV. MUTUAL RELATIONS

Behavior questions are distinct in kind from action questions—distinct, but also connected. They are connected because they are asked about the same phenomena: Why does the man hand over the discs? Nor is this connection merely external and coincidental. It embraces persistent mutual relations of considerable intricacy.

Action investigations may on occasion confine themselves to explicating systems of action without asking how the systems originated under the influence of the environment and without asking how the environment operates to transmit them and keep them in being. Likewise, some behavior investigations may confine themselves to questions about the origin and maintenance of various features of behavior without asking how the conceptual setting of those features is to be explicated.

Even so the two sorts of investigations, like the two sorts of questions, are normally complementary. Where one sort ends, space opens up for the other sort to begin. Very often, moreover, the one sort invites the attention of the other by encroaching far enough on its domain to start up questions there. An action investigation moves easily and naturally from explicating the concepts and rules embodied in certain actions to discussing the activities of learning and teaching those concepts and rules. A behavior investigation often begins with gestures at explication (sometimes more than gestures). A complex action may need to be analyzed into its components before one can say how it is built up by reinforcements; the reinforcements may have to be looked for in an environment itself constituted by concepts and rules.

As Skinner recognizes, the environment to be invoked in explanations of human behavior is a social as well as a physical one. The actions of other people—cooperating or obstructing; praising or blaming; rewarding or failing to reward—provide positive and negative reinforcements that shape behavior. So long as action investigations take the functions of such actions into account, and so long as behavior investigations ascribe such functions to actions, a continuing basis for partnership will exist.

The resulting partnership may be very intimate. As we have seen, inspecting the discs and handing them back is an action in a repertoire that contains other actions. If the items in the repertoire are all described—even explicated—as actions, and the reinforcements shaping the repertoire are also so described—as actions, for instance, of the foreman and the other workers—then only the evolutionary scheme of explanation would distinguish the investigation from a pure action investigation. The scheme would be the scheme of a behavior explanation, but the items filling it out would all be actions, explicated to a greater or lesser degree.[5]

## V. PARALLEL SCIENTIFIC FEATURES

There are other reasons, besides an ever-present basis for mutually profitable partnership, why behavior investigations and action investigations deserve each other's attention. It is important to notice that they are capable of being equally empirical. The intuitive assessments of inner life which Skinner, on the one side, would dispense with can be dispensed with on the other side too. Indeed in the end they have to be dispensed with. If an action investigator had a hunch that a certain action meant "inspected and rejected," could he offer the hunch in evidence? His colleagues would surely wonder why the hunch had not been tested by further observations. Intuition is not an optional way of establishing the significance of actions or the content of concepts and norms any more than it is an optional way of establishing the effects of various reinforcements. It is no way at all: at most it is a way of initiating investigations, which have to be brought to an end by public observation and public reasoning.[6]

Justifying Popper's confidence in the unity of method as he characterizes it, behavior investigations and action investigations call with equal strength for accumulating knowledge step by step by producing hypotheses and testing deductions from them. An anthropologist trying to discover the kinship system of an unfamiliar tribe makes successive hypotheses—more and more comprehensive attempts at formulating the rules—until he hits upon one from which none of the cases seems to escape. Economists studying decision making elaborate a model that seems consonant with the concepts and norms associated with economic actions in their own society.

[5] Such an explanation would more than satisfy Schutz's requirement that scientific constructions in social science maintain their connections with "the real social life-world" (see p. 58 and p. 67 below).

[6] Cf. the comments on intuition by Popper and Schumpeter (see below, pp. 36–39 and pp. 115–118).

To see whether it does fit, they must (in effect) hypothesize that it does, and consider how the evidence falls in with the testable consequences of that hypothesis.

Behavior explanations and action explanations resemble one another, furthermore, in being equally relevant to controlling and predicting social phenomena. To know what norms a man is likely to be acting under is a good basis for predicting that he will do some sorts of things and not others; to know what concepts are familiar to him indicates what sorts of appeals and arguments might move him to do one action rather than another. If the object of science (as people often say, thinking of social science, too) is prediction and control, then action investigations are just as scientific as behavior investigations—though their scientific status does not rest solely on that narrow conception of science. Action investigations may even give quicker results: for it may be much easier to modify a person's conduct by appealing to concepts and rules than to recondition him by setting up new basic schedules of reinforcement.

Finally, though the full scope of this possibility may be less easy to discern, action explanations as well as behavior explanations are susceptible of formal and mathematical treatment. For example, mathematical logic offers means for exactly and perspicuously representing the connections of concepts and the systematic interdependence of social rules, though special developments in the logic of norms [7] have not yet been given the widespread application in social science which they are suited to.

Mathematics of other kinds has a ready application to at least some action questions, most prominently those of pure economic theory. The standard treatment of rational choice in economic theory—as illustrated in Simon's discussion (see p. 84 ff. below)— refines such concepts as "thrift," "efficiency," and "prudence"; and simultaneously elaborates the rules laying down criteria for the application of these concepts. In their ordinary use, the concepts are concerned with actions that involve the management of quantities: with getting one's money's worth; with making one's efforts (or expenditures) count for as much as possible; with making sure that the amounts spent on present purchases do not exhaust funds

[7] See various writings by Alan R. Anderson, especially his article (with Omar K. Moore), "The Formal Analysis of Normative Concepts," *American Sociological Review* (February 1957), pp. 9–17.

that need to be saved for future ones. Correspondingly, the idealized version of choice and action elaborated in pure economic theory is permeated with mathematical thinking, as Simon's discussion makes sufficiently clear.

## VI. LARGER-SCALE INVESTIGATIONS

How much application is there for the behavior-action principle of sorting outside the elementary subject matter of the social sciences? This question has already been partly answered. We have seen that inquiries into the meaning of one person's actions open up investigations of the concepts that he shares in interaction with other people. These investigations in their turn lead to attempts at characterizing the context of concepts and rules—the culture—within which particular actions and sequences of interaction take place. We have also seen that inquiries into the origin of items in one person's repertoire of behavior open up investigations of the reinforcements which people supply to each other. *These* investigations lead to attempts at tracing the evolution of social institutions and whole societies within given environments.

Some investigations carried on by social scientists do not, however, belong to these ramifications on either the behavior or the action side. Statistical investigations in quest of quantitative correlations do not figure very prominently in the departments of social science—for example, anthropology and legal studies—which concentrate most emphatically on the systematic explication of concepts and norms. On the other hand, how many statistical investigations are concerned with correlations between reinforcements and probabilities of behavior? Many of them proceed with other schemes of explanation in mind, schemes that may be natural-scientific in conception without by any means being identical with an evolutionary scheme like Skinner's.

The proportion of power-hungry people who obtain public office may perhaps be correlated with the degree to which political institutions are (by some set of measures) centralized. Again, the number of unskilled workers who rise into top management circles may be found to decline with long-run increases in the amount of capital goods (equipment) used per worker. In neither of these cases would statistical findings identify reinforcements, repertoires, or items in repertoires; nor would they identify actions, concepts, or norms.

Some statistical findings may be destined to figure in schemes of explanation that abstract from the actions and behavior of single persons. Schemes of this sort may content themselves with establishing mathematical relationships between variables that sum up different aspects of the economic activities of an entire country. In the basic post-Keynesian scheme for explaining how the size of the national income is determined, all the variables are countrywide totals—total investment, total consumption, and total income. None can be identified as reinforcements or as items in an organism's repertoire. In a capitalistic or mixed economy, none can be said to explicate concepts or rules that are expressed in the actions of single agents or agencies. In this case, action considerations or behavior considerations would come into play only if one descended below the level of countrywide totals—to ask, for example,[8] not just how the totals were mutually related, but how one or another of them is built up.

Many statistical investigations and many large-scale schemes of explanation may thus escape the grasp of the principle. Nevertheless, the behavior-action principle does have useful applications to larger-scale investigations beyond indicating how some of them ramify out of investigations of the actions and behavior of single persons. Social science studies among other things the careers and policies of *organizations*—political, economic, both or neither—whose constitutions, programs, and activities often persist through changes in personnel. As decision-making units, organizations bear an analogy to single persons, and the analogy furnishes models for conceptualizing the activity of organizations. (It is, regrettably, an analogy that may create darkness as well as light. Applied to the state, it has often created mystery in political philosophy. Applied to any organization, it demands close precautionary attention to the variety of possible relations between group activities and the activities of group members. See the selection from Allport, p. 27 below.)

Two sorts of models for decision-making units emerge from the analogy, embodying different plans for constructing descriptions of their activity: behavior-models and action-models. A behavior investigation of a business firm—an important and representative type of organization—will treat the firm as analogous to an organism; it will ask, in effect, how the repertoire of actions and policies exhibited by the firm evolved in adaptation to its environment. In the

[8] As Keynes himself, of course, did ask. See below, p. 116, footnote 5.

past, the firm will have attempted some sorts of activities that it found unprofitable or otherwise troublesome; it will have attempted other sorts sufficiently successful to be repeated among its continuing policies. The form into which a behavior explanation casts such findings is the form of saying, the firm discards actions and policies that are not reinforced and retains actions and policies that are.

By contrast, an action investigation of the firm would envisage the firm as a purposeful—planful—agent operating together with other economic agents in a context of rules for doing business. What conceptions of business policy manifest themselves in the firm's budgeting and accounting procedures, or in its methods of recruiting? What rules does it use for deciding whether to start up or shut down another production line? To build up or draw down inventories? Besides asking questions like these, an action investigation might expand into an attempt to set forth both the announced conventions of the particular markets in which the firm operates— for example, the customary credit arrangements—and the tacit conventions under which the firm may share its markets with major competitors.

## VII. ACTION AND PRESCRIPTION

Investigations of the kind just mentioned belong, equally with the behavior investigations mentioned previously, to what is traditionally called "institutional economics." (The behavior-action principle thus sorts *within* this field.) Another vehicle for answering action questions is the pure theory of the firm, which explains what a firm would do if it were an ideally rational agent seeking to budget its resources so as to minimize costs and seeking to regulate its output so as to maximize profits. The theory thus does for certain organizations what a parallel theory of consumer choice does for single persons: it provides an idealized explication (and elaboration) of the concepts and norms that define the rational management of efforts and resources.[9]

As an elaboration of concepts and norms actually found in use

[9] The technical refinements which the theory of the firm introduces into the basic action-model will be familiar to students of economics. The refinements issue in proofs, for example, (1) that budgets will be less than perfect if they deviate from the rule that the same returns must be obtained from equal marginal expenditures on different resources; (2) that the best rule for production is to carry it on to the point at which marginal cost equals marginal revenue, and no farther. Cf. Simon on the firm, p. 85 ff. below.

and needing explication, the theory of the firm has a descriptive function. It is descriptive, too, insofar as it may be held to portray the efficiency in action and policy to which economic agents may be forced if they find themselves in unremitting competition with other agents. (In such circumstances, behavior investigations would show that only maximally efficient actions were likely to be reinforced.)

The theory also sets up a model for organizations to imitate, whether or not they are forced to. If an organization sets out to be rational and efficient and prudent in the use of its resources—whatever these may be, money, land, people, influence—then the pure theory of rational action (of which the theory of the firm is simply one representative branch) prescribes that it must exactly match its resources to its opportunities. To find an optimum set of policies, it must size up what it wants to do, in order of urgency; reckon what can be done, given its situation, with the resources at its command; and apportion every quantum of resources so that each is given the best possible use.

But can organizations hope to calculate optimum solutions of this kind? In the real world, organizations of all sorts—including the typical firm, as well as the state—operate under severe limitations respecting information. They cannot obtain that comprehensive view of their situation and their resources which the idealized theory of rational action assumes; if they spent (impossibly large) amounts of time and money with the hope of getting a close approximation to such a view, they would find it out-of-date if they got near it. The world does not stand still. Organizations cannot in practice even come to the end of discovering their own aims. Within firms—and even more so, within democratic organizations—there are continual problems about reconciling conflicting (and shifting) personal preferences.

If the model prescribed by the pure theory of rational action cannot be carried out, then organizations will have to carry on policy-making some other way. Popper (see pp. 99–107 below) suggests that they follow the model of "piecemeal social engineering," limiting themselves to small moves designed to correct outstanding difficulties, and moving further only when it is clear what the results were of previous moves. Policies would thus advance step by step with the lessons to be drawn from policies. Instead of grandiose experiments whose results cannot be sorted out, this approach to policy formation would offer experiments small enough for the results to be accurately traced—with possibly the further advantage of multiplying the number of experiments, since, on this approach, policy formation might devolve piece by piece on a plurality of organizations, private as well as public (cf. pp. 103–105 below).

Taken descriptively, the model of piecemeal social engineering seems to belong to the series of transformations that according to Simon (see p. 88 ff. below) lead from "optimizing" models of behavior to "adaptive" models. Thus prescriptions elaborated in the action branch of social science are kept in check by descriptive considerations drawn from the behavior branch.

## VIII. THE IDEOLOGICAL PREDICAMENT

However, how much will be gained in realism either for science or for policy making by changing models in this way? Some people may nourish extravagant hopes, which only the pure theory of rational action would sanction, of planning in optimum detail all the business of an ideal society. But do not other people fall short of understanding how many social improvements lie within their reach? They may be especially liable to falling short when to exert themselves in vision or policy might cost them (and people like them) something uncomfortably large in privileges, status, or power.

Social scientists who accept the model of piecemeal social engineering may thus do so less for its greater realism than for its ideological convenience. Marxists charge that the ubiquitous tendency of Western social scientists to dissolve large social processes into interactions of plural groups reflects an ideological refusal to confront the paramount facts of the class struggle. The compatibility between piecemeal engineering and social pluralism would in this light only feed the suspicions aroused by the main stresses of the piecemeal doctrine. What, it might be asked, is this emphasis on small departures but a way of slowing down social change? How many of the necessities that must be adapted to so carefully are merely contingent social institutions (like private property) that could be done away with?

Ideology constitutes a predicament more insidious than the universal liability of mankind to personal prejudice. Social scientists can correct each other on points of personal prejudice, in which one man deviates from his colleagues—but how can they correct for a pervasive bias that they all may share, because they belong to a given society and enjoy similar privileges within it?

The predicament is not confined to piecemeal social engineering. The Utopian visions that people—reactionaries as well as revolutionaries—have had of thoroughly planned republics have not failed to reflect class interests and class prejudices. But the predicament broadens beyond class interests. It infects the outlook of whole societies. How much objective truth can social scientists attain about their own society and culture, sharing its dominant prejudices? How fair are they likely to be to the different outlooks of other societies?

Behavior investigations are perhaps less liable to distortion than action investigations. They may exaggerate the limitations of the environment; but they are at least ready to recognize the possibility of changes within these limitations, and they have a firm quantitative apparatus to fall back on that assists the process of objective analysis and criticism which Schumpeter invokes to keep ideology under control (see pp. 108–118 below). Whereas action investigations easily degenerate into complacent and self-limiting recitations of cultural peculiarities: they readily impute to the fabric of the world the concepts and norms associated with contingent social arrangements; and in spite of the lessons to be found in history and anthropology find it difficult to envisage any basic variations on these arrangements.

Yet action investigations, too, may invoke Schumpeter's methods of control, which consist essentially in pursuing the inherent dialectic of scientific ambitions. Here, too, in the explication of concepts and norms, the exchange of criticism constantly intensifies the demand for more and more precise schemes of explanation fitted to wider and wider reaches of fact. Ideological distortions will give way before the drive to meet this demand. (But how far and how fast?)

## IX. SOCIAL SCIENCE AND PHILOSOPHY

Philosophy, like social science, runs the risks of the ideological predicament. Explicating the concepts and relations between concepts familiar to a given culture, philosophers may convert optional moral rules into natural moral laws and make metaphysical theses out of their own contingent habits of thought. It has been charged, for instance, that the metaphysical distinction between substance and accident rests on nothing more than the grammatical peculiarities of Indo-European languages. According to a view now very widespread in English-speaking countries,[10] though still controversial, philosophy not only needs to investigate such charges; it does best to conceive all philosophical problems as problems about language. On the other hand, some philosophers who have accepted this conception—those who occupy themselves with untangling the usages of ordinary language—have been accused in their turn of abandoning the search for permanent truths in favor of perpetuating the dubious (unscientific) commonplaces of their own time and milieu.

Everyone will agree that the investigation of concepts is philosophical business. Concepts, however, manifest themselves in language—in speech-acts; their characteristics can be observed publicly only by observing how the words that represent them are used. Unlike a philologist, a philosopher will primarily be interested, not in the historical peculiarities of given languages, nor in theories about their historical development, but in logical features of usage that might be paralleled (more or less conveniently) in any of an unlimited variety of languages. But the domain of philosophy is still, on this view, the domain of a social phenomenon: the received apparatus of concepts, simultaneously manifested in a number of languages, with which men carry on their activities in the world (including the activities of social science)—an apparatus that for each culture or linguistic community represents at the same time the most important product of social interaction and the most important instrument for facilitating it.

On this view, further developed, philosophical investigations become a species of action investigations, especially concerned with characterizing the varieties of speech-acts that initiate (and bring to an end) distinct activities of inquiry. Thus a philosopher concerns himself with explicating the differences between moral questions and aesthetic questions; or with explaining what concepts and rules govern accepted acts of explanation in social science.

The fact that philosophy is an activity of inquiry dealing with other activities of inquiry—thus operating at one remove from *some* of the activities which social science inquires into—should not be allowed to obscure the fact that in other respects the work

[10] Illustrated by the selections from Carnap and Black in a companion volume to the present one, Henry W. Johnstone, Jr., (ed.), *What Is Philosophy?* (New York: The Macmillan Co., 1965).

is the same as that of action investigations. The speech-acts that philosophers explicate are genuine actions. When philosophers propound theses of explication, other philosophers confront them with counterexamples—observed or observable usages that tend to falsify the explications. The theses are then revised; and tested again. The methods of philosophy, therefore, as well as the phenomena it deals with, fall within the embrace of social science.

Does it demean philosophy to be found there? One might as sensibly ask, does it demean social science? The embrace is a mutual one. In its action branch, social science keeps company with the humanities. Is not the meaning of human actions their common concern? The selection below (pp. 80–82) from James Agee demonstrates simultaneously what a novelist can do if he has the tasks of a social scientist; and what a social scientist can do if he has the sensitivity of a novelist.

The ideological predicament forestalls any *general* vindication for philosophy either as a social science or as a humanity. Every investigation and every explanation must be examined for itself. But philosophy, like social science, can cope with the predicament by developing ever higher standards of precision and meeting tests drawn from ever wider observations. The statement that the behavior-action principle of sorting assigns some questions, investigations, and explanations to the behavior side and some to the action side, while others sort out neither way, was equally a thesis in philosophy and a hypothesis in social science. Some tests have been performed on it in this Introduction. The readings that follow will suggest further tests as they suggest further ways of elaborating the hypothesis; and the world of social science lies open before those who would provide for its judicious application.

B. F. SKINNER

# Is a Science of Human Behavior Possible?

*Many social scientists would perhaps claim the name of "science" only in a prospective sense—signifying not so much what they have accomplished to date, but rather what they hope to accomplish in the future. Hopes as well as accomplishments, however, confront the same familiar doubts and misgivings. In the following selection, Skinner offers an expeditious treatment of some recurrent objections.*

*B. F. Skinner (1904–    ), professor of psychology at Harvard, is renowned both for his militant behaviorism, which insists that human beings behave like other organisms, and for his experimental skill, which induces other organisms to behave like human beings.*

Behavior is not one of those subject matters which become accessible only with the invention of an instrument such as the telescope or microscope. We all know thousands of facts about behavior. Actually there is no subject matter with which we could be better acquainted, for we are always in the presence of at least one behaving organism. But this familiarity is something of a disadvantage, for it means that we have probably jumped to conclusions which will not be supported by the cautious methods of science. Even though we have observed behavior for many years, we are not necessarily able, without help, to express useful uniformities or lawful relations. We may show considerable skill in making plausible guesses about what our friends and acquaintances will do under various circumstances or what we ourselves will do. We may make plausible generalizations about the conduct of people in general. But very few of these will survive careful analysis. A great deal of unlearning generally takes place in our early contact with a science of behavior.

Behavior is a difficult subject matter, not because it is inaccessible, but because it is extremely complex. Since it is a process, rather than a thing, it cannot easily be held still for observation. It is

Reprinted with permission of the publisher from *Science and Human Behavior*, pp. 14–22, by B. F. Skinner. Copyright 1953 by The Macmillan Company.

19

changing, fluid, and evanescent, and for this reason it makes great technical demands upon the ingenuity and energy of the scientist. But there is nothing essentially insoluble about the problems which arise from this fact.

Several kinds of statements about behavior are commonly made. When we tell an anecdote or pass along a bit of gossip, we report a *single event*—what someone did upon such and such an occasion: "She slammed the door and walked off without a word." Our report is a small bit of history. History itself is often nothing more than similar reporting on a broad scale. The biographer often confines himself to a series of episodes in the life of his subject. The case history, which occupies an important place in several fields of psychology, is a kind of biography which is also concerned mainly with what a particular person did at particular times and places: "When she was eleven, Mary went to live with her maiden aunt in Winchester." Novels and short stories may be thought of as veiled biography or history, since the ingredients of even a highly fanciful work of fiction are somehow or other taken from life. The narrative reporting of the behavior of people at particular times and places is also part of the sciences of archeology, ethnology, sociology, and anthropology.

These accounts have their uses. They broaden the experience of those who have not had firsthand access to similar data. But they are only the beginnings of a science. No matter how accurate or quantitative it may be, the report of the single case is only a preliminary step. The next step is the discovery of some sort of *uniformity*. When we tell an anecdote to support an argument, or report a case history to exemplify a principle, we imply a general rule, no matter how vaguely it may be expressed. The historian is seldom content with mere narration. He reports his facts to support a theory—of cycles, trends, or patterns of history. In doing so he passes from the single instance to the rule. When a biographer traces the influence of an early event upon a man's later life, he transcends simple reporting and asserts, no matter how hesitantly, that one thing has caused another. Fable and allegory are more than storytelling if they imply some kind of uniformity in human behavior, as they generally do. Our preference for "consistency of character" and our rejection of implausible coincidences in literature show that we expect lawfulness. The "manners" and "customs" of the sociologist and anthropologist report the *general* behavior of groups of people.

A vague sense of order emerges from any sustained observation of human behavior. Any plausible guess about what a friend will do or say in a given circumstance is a prediction based upon some such uniformity. If a reasonable order was not discoverable, we could scarcely be effective in dealing with human affairs. The methods of science are designed to clarify these uniformities and make them explicit. The techniques of field study of the anthropologist and social psychologist, the procedures of the psychological clinic, and the controlled experimental methods of the laboratory are all directed toward this end, as are also the mathematical and logical tools of science.

Many people interested in human behavior do not feel the need for the standards of proof characteristic of an exact science; the uniformities in behavior are "obvious" without them. At the same time, they are reluctant to accept the conclusions toward which such proof inescapably points if they do not "sense" the uniformity themselves. But these idiosyncrasies are a costly luxury. We need not defend the methods of science in their application to behavior. The experimental and mathematical techniques used in discovering and expressing uniformities are the common property of science in general. Almost every discipline has contributed to this pool of resources, and all disciplines borrow from it. The advantages are well established.

## SOME OBJECTIONS TO A SCIENCE OF BEHAVIOR

The report of a single event raises no theoretical problems and comes into no conflict with philosophies of human behavior. The scientific laws or systems which express uniformities are likely to conflict with theory because they claim the same territory. When a science of behavior reaches the point of dealing with lawful relationships, it meets the resistance of those who give their allegiance to prescientific or extrascientific conceptions. The resistance does not always take the form of an overt rejection of science. It may be transmuted into claims of limitations, often expressed in highly scientific terms.

It has sometimes been pointed out, for example, that physical science has been unable to maintain its philosophy of determinism, particularly at the subatomic level. The Principle of Indeterminacy states that there are circumstances under which the physicist cannot put himself in possession of all relevant information: if he chooses to observe one event, he must relinquish the possibility of observing another. In our present state of knowledge, certain events therefore appear to be unpredictable. It does not follow that these events are free or capricious. Since human behavior is enormously complex and the human organism is of limited dimensions, many acts may involve processes to which the Principle of Indeterminacy applies. It does not follow that human behavior is free, but only that it may be beyond the range of a predictive or controlling science. Most students of behavior, however, would be willing to settle for the degree of prediction and control achieved by the physical sciences in spite of this limitation. A final answer to the problem of lawfulness is to be sought, not in the limits of any hypothetical mechanism within the organism, but in our ability to demonstrate lawfulness in the behavior of the organism as a whole.

A similar objection has a logical flavor. It is contended that reason cannot comprehend itself or—in somewhat more substantial terms— that the behavior required in understanding one's own behavior must be something beyond the behavior which is understood. It is true that knowledge is limited by the limitations of the knowing organism. The number of things in the world which might be known certainly exceeds the number of possible different states in all possible knowers. But the laws and systems of science are designed to make a knowledge of particular events unimportant. It is by no means necessary that one man should understand all the facts in a given field, but only that he should understand all the *kinds* of facts. We have no reason to suppose that the human intellect is incapable of formulating or comprehending the basic principles of human behavior—certainly not until we have a clearer notion of what those principles are.

The assumption that behavior is a lawful scientific datum sometimes meets with another objection. Science is concerned with the general, but the behavior of the individual is necessarily unique. The "case history" has a richness and flavor which are in decided contrast with general principles. It is easy to convince oneself that there are two distinct worlds and that one is beyond the reach of science. This distinction is not peculiar to the study of behavior. It can always be made in the early stages of any science, when it is not clear what we may deduce from a general principle with respect to a particular case. What the science of physics has to say about the world is dull and colorless to the beginning student when compared with his daily experience, but he later discovers that it is actually a more incisive account of even the single instance. When we wish to deal effectively with the single instance, we turn to science for help. The argument will lose cogency as a science of behavior progresses and as the implications of its general laws become clear. A comparable argument against the possibility of a science of medicine has already lost its significance. In *War and Peace,* Tolstoy wrote of the illness of a favorite character as follows:

> Doctors came to see Natasha, both separately and in consultation. They said a great deal in French, in German, and in Latin. They criticised one another, and prescribed the most diverse remedies for all the diseases they were familiar with. But it never occurred to one of them to make the simple reflection that they could not understand the disease from which Natasha was suffering, as no single disease can be fully understood in a living person; for every living person has his individual peculiarities and always has his own peculiar, new, complex complaints unknown to medicine—not a disease of the lungs, of the kidneys, of the skin, of the heart, and so on, as described in medical books, but a disease that consists of one out of the innumerable combinations of ailments of those organs.

Tolstoy was justified in calling every sickness a unique event. Every action of the individual is unique, as well as every event in physics and chemistry. But his objection to a science of medicine in terms of uniqueness was unwarranted. The argument was plausible enough at the time; no one could then contradict him by supplying the necessary general principles. But a great deal has happened in medical science since then, and today few people would care to argue that a disease cannot be described in general terms or that a single case cannot be discussed by referring to factors common to many cases. The intuitive wisdom of the old-style diagnostician has been largely replaced by the analytical procedures of the clinic, just as a scientific analysis of behavior will eventually replace the personal interpretation of unique instances.

A similar argument is leveled at the use of statistics in a science of behavior. A prediction of what the *average* individual will do is often of little or no value in dealing with a particular individual. The actuarial tables of life-insurance companies are of no value to a physician in predicting the death or survival of a particular patient. This issue is still alive in the physical sciences, where it is associated with the concepts of causality and probability. It is seldom that the science of physics deals with the behavior of individual molecules, atoms, or subatomic particles. When it is occasionally called upon to do so, all the problems of the particular event arise. In general a science is helpful in dealing with the individual only insofar as its laws refer to individuals. A science of behavior which concerns only the behavior of groups is not likely to be of help in our understanding of the particular case. But a science may also deal with the behavior of the individual, and its success in doing so must be evaluated in terms of its achievements rather than any a priori contentions.

The extraordinary complexity of behavior is sometimes held to be an added source of difficulty. Even though behavior may be lawful, it may be too complex to be dealt with in terms of law. Sir Oliver Lodge [1] once asserted that "though an astronomer can calculate the orbit of a planet or comet or even a meteor, although a physicist can deal with the structure of atoms, and a chemist with their possible combinations, neither a biologist nor any scientific man can calculate the orbit of a common fly." This is a statement about the limitations of scientists or about their aspirations, not about the suitability of a subject matter. Even so, it is wrong. It may be said with some assurance that if no one has calculated the orbit of a fly, it is only because no one has been sufficiently interested in doing so. The tropistic movements of many insects are now fairly well understood, but the instrumentation needed to record the flight of a fly and to give an account of all the conditions affecting it would cost more than the importance of the subject justifies. There is, therefore, no reason to conclude, as the author does, that "an incalculable element of self-determination thus makes its appearance quite low down the animal scale." Self-determination does not follow from complexity. Difficulty in calculating the orbit of the fly does not prove capriciousness, though it may make it impossible to prove anything else. The problems imposed by the complexity of a subject matter must be dealt with as they arise. Apparently hopeless cases often become manageable in time. It is only recently that any sort of lawful account of the weather has been possible. We often succeed in reducing complexity to a reasonable degree by simplifying conditions in the laboratory; but where this is impossible, a statistical analysis may be used to achieve an inferior, but in many ways

[1] British physicist (1851–1940).—Ed.

acceptable, prediction. Certainly no one is prepared to say now what a science of behavior can or cannot accomplish eventually. Advance estimates of the limits of science have generally proved inaccurate. The issue is in the long run pragmatic: we cannot tell until we have tried.

Still another objection to the use of scientific method in the study of human behavior is that behavior is an anomalous subject matter because a prediction made about it may alter it. If we tell a friend that he is going to buy a particular kind of car, he may react to our prediction by buying a different kind. The same effect has been used to explain the failures of public opinion polls. In the presidential election of 1948 it was confidently predicted that a majority of the voters would vote for a candidate who, as it turned out, lost the election. It has been asserted that the electorate reacted to the prediction in a contrary way and that the published prediction therefore had an effect upon the predicted event. But it is by no means necessary that a prediction of behavior be permitted to affect the behaving individual. There may have been practical reasons why the results of the poll in question could not be withheld until after the election, but this would not be the case in a purely scientific endeavor.

There are other ways in which observer and observed interact. Study distorts the thing studied. But there is no special problem here peculiar to human behavior. It is now accepted as a general principle in scientific method that it is necessary to interfere in some degree with any phenomenon in the act of observing it. A scientist may have an effect upon behavior in the act of observing or analyzing it, and he must certainly take this effect into account. But behavior may also be observed with a minimum of interaction between subject and scientist, and this is the case with which one naturally tries to begin.

A final objection deals with the practical application of a scientific analysis. Even if we assume that behavior is lawful and that the methods of science will reveal the rules which govern it, we may be unable to make any technological use of these rules unless certain conditions can be brought under control. In the laboratory many conditions are simplified and irrelevant conditions often eliminated. But of what value are laboratory studies if we must predict and control behavior where a comparable simplification is impossible? It is true that we can gain control over behavior only insofar as we can control the factors responsible for it. What a scientific study does is to enable us to make optimal use of the control we possess. The laboratory simplification reveals the relevance of factors which we might otherwise overlook.

We cannot avoid the problems raised by a science of behavior by simply denying that the necessary conditions can be controlled. In actual fact there is a considerable degree of control over many relevant conditions. In penal institutions and military organizations the control is extensive. We control the environment of the human organism in the nursery and in institutions which care for those to whom the conditions of the nursery remain necessary in later life. Fairly extensive control of conditions relevant to human behavior is maintained in industry in the form of wages and conditions of work, in schools in the form of grades and conditions of work, in commerce by anyone in possession of goods or money, by governmental agencies through the police and military, in the psychological clinic through the consent of the controllee, and so on. A degree of effective control, not so easily identified, rests in the hands of entertainers, writers, advertisers, and propagandists. These controls, which are often all too evident in their practical application, are more than sufficient to permit us to extend the results of a laboratory science to the interpretation of human behavior in daily affairs—for either theoretical or practical purposes. Since a science of behavior will continue to increase the effective use of this control, it is now more important than ever to understand the processes involved and to prepare ourselves for the problems which will certainly arise.

FLOYD H. ALLPORT

# Logical Complexities of Group Activity

*Besides the activities of individual human beings in social contexts, social science investigates the activities of human groups. Groups and their activities may be regarded as constituted by numbers of people acting together. But how together and how constituted? There is a perennial philosophical problem—or family of problems—about how wholes are logically constructed out of parts. Do wholes have any properties that cannot be reduced to properties of their parts? The question that Allport deals with is even more fundamental: Is there any unique way of conceiving the construction of a given whole?*

*Floyd H. Allport (1890–    ), now retired, was professor of social and political psychology at Syracuse University for many years. His book* Social Psychology *(Boston: Houghton Mifflin & Co., 1924) was an early standard work in the field. It was reviewed in 1926 by L. L. Bernard (1881–1951), an American sociologist; the following selection is drawn from a comment that Allport was asked to make on the review in 1961.*

Let me try to show . . . why the problem of defining 'group action' has proved so slippery. We need some sort of paradigm; and I will choose, for the purpose, the structuring of the action of a 'team' in a football game. First, let us consider the moment after the kickoff, when the 'group action' might be described economically by saying that 'the team runs down the field.' Here we see a number of individuals *doing essentially the same thing* as part of a larger situation. The paradigm can be readily generalized to apply to innumerable instances, such as factory workers operating 'in parallel' at the same type of machines, soldiers marching abreast, or church-goers listening to a sermon. Bernard's remark that sociologists have simply applied individual terminology "to uniformities of behavior in groups as wholes" seems not inappropriate here. To say that the *'team'* runs down the field, though useful, does, however, imply a personification and a specious singularity.

Suppose now that forward pass occurs. Instead of saying the

From Floyd H. Allport, "The Contemporary Appraisal of an Old Problem," *Contemporary Psychology*, VI (June 1961), pp. 195–196. Copyright 1961 by the American Psychological Association, Inc. Used by permission of the American Psychological Association and the author.

team runs down the field, we say that the team 'executes a forward pass.' Here Bernard's formulation misses the characteristic element of the structural format altogether. The situation is not composed of 'uniformities' but of differences. One man drops back and throws, another catches, dodges, and runs, still another blocks, and so on. There is, literally, *no* individual who carries out the act that we have attributed to the team, *viz.*, the 'execution of a forward pass.'

Since we are unable to describe the forward pass episode as an act of an individual, suppose that we call it an act of the group. The 'team' carries out the play. Here, at the social level, we have again invented through the term *team* a useful singularity. This phase of the paradigm extrapolates to limitless examples of 'wholes' of *differentiated* but *integrated* activities. The 'corporate fiction' is something without which our economic, political, and organizational life in general could hardly go on. But the trouble here, from the standpoint of objective science, is that the term for the agency which is said to 'execute the forward pass' is devoid of any unambiguously denotable referent. When we try to touch or speak to the 'team,' we are encountering or addressing only individuals. The corporate fiction, though a useful orienting device for perceiving and handling a situation in a certain way, is still a fiction.

Does this mean that the whole matter of 'collective reality' is an illusion? By no means. For one thing, we note that the ball has actually been advanced. I challenge anyone to show how, in the context of these conditions, this could have happened through the act of an individual without concurrent acts of other individuals. There is 'collective action' certainly, but we have not learned how to conceptualize it. There is a lack of unambiguous explicit denotation when we attribute an action to the 'corporate entity' *team*. This inadequacy can also be looked at from another angle. Not only is the 'team,' *as such*, not here explicitly encounterable; it is represented conceptually, by implication, as a (single) thing, an 'agent' that takes a singular verb ('executes'). We know, however, that *many* acts, acts of a *number* of different explicit entities (individuals), are involved. The important consideration is that all these acts, in principle, are necessary: a *plural* number of elements is *required* in the collective act of the forward pass. We are not denying the idea of 'unity of operation' of the 'team.' But to state *what the team is in itself* surely calls for the retaining and stressing of the idea of plurality in our defining concept. Failure to do so is tantamount to selling out our 'pure science' interest in the problem for the sake of practical expediency.

But let us carry our paradigm still further. Consider the various nuances of the term when we say that the *team* advances the ball,' that it 'is penalized,' that it 'wins the trophy,' that it is 'under contract,' that it 'is transported to its game in a bus,' that it 'eats at a training table.' These changing images of the team, based largely upon how the individuals are involved, arise from the fact that an individual's person or behavior is usually not totally, but only partially, included in any of the groupings of which he is a member. This is true even to the extent of allowing him to belong to a number of 'groups' simultaneously.

An equally significant shift occurs according to the topological position of the observer. Consider, for example, the quarterback's (inside) imagery of 'the team,' near the opponents' goal line, as he considers the strategic placement and action of each player in connection with the others. Compare this imagery with the (outside) meaning of 'the team' as experienced by the rooter when he is shouting, "Touchdown, Syracuse!" It is well to realize that this difference of point of view (inside or outside) toward what we are observing controls our potential experience or conceptualization of all 'entities' of nature, from the 'neutron' and 'atom,' through 'organism' and 'personality,' to 'nations' and 'nation-coalitions.' In addition, therefore, to their having ambiguous denotation, misleading singularity, and shifting character, group concepts are *relative* concepts.

The reader can now judge for himself whether my concern over the lack of critical attention to the designations used for societal realities was exaggerated. My view on this matter has not changed, but I now see the problem more broadly. It now seems to me both more fundamental and more difficult. It is not a matter merely of eschewing a certain dubious terminology, but of critical overhauling of the underlying concepts. There are doubtless some who would protest that this is not really necessary, for social science is, and will remain, a teleological rather than a 'pure science enterprise.' Disinterested science can deal with the lower orders, but at the societal level something new 'emerges' that must inevitably color our conceptualizations. To these I would reply that, if they are going to attribute our ineptitude in dealing with the collective problem to teleology, they will have to carry their belief in teleological causation further down in the hierarchy of nature than even they would wish. The issue we have been discussing extends more deeply than to the societal or even to the biological level. It is disconcerting to realize that what I have pointed out about the instability and uncertainty of concepts of collective entity is no more true when applied to groups than when applied to that mysterious assembly we call an individual. We see that psychologists have had to decide, somewhat arbitrarily, between the 'molar' and 'molecular' view of the individual, with different consequences as to the phenomena studied. Even at the submicroscopic order, though the atom (taken as a whole) appears to be *entirely* made up of such 'entities' as electrons, protons, and neutrons, and their motions, the view we have of 'atoms' (externally) and what they do differs notably from the way we conceptualize these subatomic realities and their relationships. As in the case of the 'group,' what we see or conceive as the 'entity' is relative to the coarseness or fineness of our observation or interpretation, and relative also to whether we are considering an aggregate situation as if from the 'outside' or the 'inside.' When we are in a position to work with an entity that we experience at one level, the entity as experienced by us at the other level disappears. We have never been able to identify and chart, or even to establish the existence of both levels and the structure of their connection in a single observation.

This, I would submit, is the reason why the problem of the group and the individual has proved so persistent and difficult. It is not a question of a 'societal' versus a 'natural' order, or even of the 'individual' versus the 'group.' The enigma lies in the successively included and inclusive hierarchical structure that exists universally in nature—the problem of collective reality *as such*.

We must here recognize an identity between our problem and the more general problem of a 'thing.' Just as we saw that the singularity 'team' which 'executes the forward pass' resolves into a plurality of individually interacting elements, so *any* 'entity' or 'thing,' at whatever level we find it, always seems to break down into a collectivity at a lower order. Our concepts of 'agent' and 'entity,' yes, even of 'thing' and 'particle,' are tentative in character. They are singularities (entities) only at a given order. When more finely approached they resolve into the unexplained pattern of 'structural' causality. Hence we might speak of 'thing' fictions as we speak of 'group' or 'corporate' fictions. The case is not altered even when 'individual' agents are conceived as acting in combination, in so-called multiple causation. An analysis *via* the part-whole problem leads to the same conclusion. A 'whole' is said to be different from its 'parts' or even from their summation. Yet, since it is made up *only* of these parts and cannot exist without them, the whole cannot be sharply and unambiguously distinguished as a 'thing' from the 'things' that are its parts except by a purely intellectual artifice.

As with the concept of the 'group,' we now find that the very notion of a 'thing,' instead of being distinct and absolute, is shifting, ambiguous in denotation, misleading as to its singularity, overlapping, relativistic, and blurred. Our understanding of 'group' realities depends, therefore, on our finding some suitable substitute for our present concept of an entity or thing. But since a 'thing' and what it does, that is to say, the events in which it is involved, has long been one of the very pillars of our notion of causality, this realization leaves us baffled as to where to turn.

KARL R. POPPER

# Unity of Method in the Natural and Social Sciences

*If there is some chance of investigating human activities scientifically, will the plan of investigation be the same as that followed in the natural sciences? Popper holds that in leading features it will be the same. The hypothetical-deductive method followed in the natural sciences takes the lead in the social sciences, too. The wholes or objects of study dealt with will often be constructed ones, defined for theoretical purposes; but any "inside views" that theorists gain of their objects must be vindicated, in the social sciences as well as in the natural ones, by public procedures of testing. Social science no doubt has special difficulties, but in principle it is capable of discovering laws (many candidates for which will be found in the second selection from Popper, p. 99 below); and the difficulties, Popper thinks, may be counterbalanced by the advantages of "zero method models" of rationality—illustrated and discussed in detail in the selection from Simon, p. 83.*

*Karl R. Popper (1902–    ), Viennese in origin and education, has been professor of logic and scientific method at the London School of Economics since 1949. He has made major contributions both to the philosophy of science and to social and political philosophy* (Logik der Forschung [1934], *translated with new appendices as* The Logic of Scientific Discovery [London: Hutchinson University Library, 1959]; The Open Society and Its Enemies [4th ed.; London: Routledge & Kegan Paul Ltd., 1962]).

I am going to propose a doctrine of the unity of method; that is to say, the view that all theoretical or generalizing sciences make use of the same method, whether they are natural sciences or social sciences. . . .

I do not intend to assert that there are no differences whatever between the methods of the theoretical sciences of nature and of society; such differences clearly exist, even between the various

From Karl R. Popper, *The Poverty of Historicism* (London: Routledge & Kegan Paul Ltd., 1957, 2d ed., 1960; and New York: Harper Torchbooks, Harper & Row, 1964). © Karl Raimund Popper 1957, 1960. Used by permission of Routledge and the author. [Taken from pp. 130–143 of the 2d (1960) edition.]

natural sciences themselves, as well as between the various social sciences. (Compare, for example, the analysis of competitive markets and of Romance languages.) But I agree with Comte and Mill—and with many others, such as C. Menger [1]—that the methods in the two fields are fundamentally the same (though the methods I have in mind may differ from those they had in mind). The methods always consist in offering deductive causal explanations, and in testing them (by way of predictions). This has sometimes been called the hypo-thetical-deductive method,[2] or more often the method of hypothesis, for it does not achieve absolute certainty for any of the scientific statements which it tests; rather, these statements always retain the character of tentative hypotheses, even though their character of tentativeness may cease to be obvious after they have passed a great number of severe tests.

Because of their tentative or provisional character, hypotheses were considered, by most students of method, as *provisional in the sense that they have ultimately to be replaced by proved theories* (or at least by theories which can be proved to be 'highly probable', in the sense of some calculus of probabilities). I believe that this view is mistaken and that it leads to a host of entirely unnecessary difficulties. But this problem [3] is of comparatively little moment

[1] Austrian economist (1840–1921).—Ed.

[2] See V. Kraft, *Die Grundformen der wissenschaftlichen Methoden* (1925).

[3] See my *Logic of Scientific Discovery*, on which the present section is based, especially the doctrine of tests by way of deduction ('deductivism') and of the redundancy of any further 'induction', since theories always retain their hypothetical character ('hypotheticism'), and the doctrine that scientific tests are genuine attempts to falsify theories ('eliminationism'); see also the discussion of testability and falsifiability.

The opposition here pointed out, between *deductivism* and *inductivism*, corresponds in some respects to the classical distinction between *rationalism* and *empiricism*: Descartes was a deductivist, since he conceived all sciences as deductive systems, while the English empiricists, from Bacon on, all conceived the sciences as collecting observations from which generalizations are obtained by induction.

But Descartes believed that the principles, the premises of the deductive systems, must be secure and self-evident—'clear and distinct'. They are based upon the insight of reason. (They are synthetic and *a priori* valid, in Kantian language.) As opposed to this, I conceive them as tentative conjectures, or hypotheses.

These hypotheses, I contend, must be refutable in principle: it is here that I deviate from the two greatest modern deductivists, Henri Poincaré and Pierre Duhem. [See the selection from Duhem in a companion volume here. What is important is to realize that in science we are always concerned with explanations, predictions, and tests, and that the method of testing hypotheses is always the same. . . . From the hypothesis to be tested—for example, a universal law—together with some other statements which for this purpose are not considered as problematic—for example, some initial conditions—we deduce some prognosis. We then confront this prognosis, whenever possible, with the results of experimental or other observations. Agreement with them is taken as corroboration of the hypothesis, though not as final proof; clear disagreement is considered as refutation or falsification.

According to this analysis, there is no great difference between explanation, prediction and testing. The difference is not one of logical structure, but rather one of emphasis; it depends on *what*

---

to the present one, Dudley Shapere, *Philosophical Problems of Natural Science* (New York: The Macmillan Co., 1965).]

Poincaré and Duhem both recognized the impossibility of conceiving the theories of physics as inductive generalizations. They realized that the observational measurements which form the alleged starting point for the generalizations are, on the contrary, *interpretations in the light of theories*. And they rejected not only inductivism, but also the rationalistic belief in synthetic *a priori* valid principles or axioms. Poincaré interpreted them as analytically true, as definitions; Duhem interpreted them as instruments (as did Cardinal Bellarmino and Bishop Berkeley), as means for the ordering of the experimental laws. Theories thus cannot contain either true or false information: they are nothing but instruments, since they can only be convenient or inconvenient, economical or uneconomical; supple and subtle, or else creaking and crude. (Thus, Duhem says, following Berkeley, there cannot be logical reasons why two or more theories which contradict one another should not all be accepted.) I fully agree with both these great authors in rejecting inductivism as well as the belief in the synthetic *a priori* validity of physical theories. But I cannot accept their view that it is impossible to submit theoretical systems to empirical tests. Some of them are testable, I think; that is, refutable in principle; and they are therefore synthetic (rather than analytic); *empirical* (rather than *a priori*); and *informative* (rather than purely instrumental). As to Duhem's famous criticism of crucial experiments, he only shows that crucial experiments can never *prove* or establish a theory; but he nowhere shows that crucial experiments cannot *refute* a theory. Admittedly, Duhem is right when he says that we can test only huge and complex theoretical systems rather than isolated hypotheses; but if we test two such systems which differ in one hypothesis only, and if we can design experiments which refute the first system while leaving the second very well corroborated, then we may be on reasonably safe ground if we attribute the failure of the first system to that hypothesis in which it differs from the other.

*we consider to be our problem* and what we do not so consider. If it
is not our problem to find a prognosis, while we take it to be our
problem to find the initial conditions or some of the universal laws
(or both) from which we may deduce a *given* 'prognosis', then we
are looking for an *explanation* (and the given 'prognosis' becomes
our 'explicandum'). If we consider the laws and initial conditions
as given (rather than as to be found) and use them merely for
deducing the prognosis, in order to get thereby some new information, then we are trying to make a *prediction*. (This is a case in
which we *apply* our scientific results.) And if we consider one
of the premises, i.e. either a universal law or an initial condition, as
problematic, and the prognosis as something to be compared with
the results of experience, then we speak of a *test* of the problematic
premise.

The result of tests is the *selection* of hypotheses which have stood
up to tests, or the *elimination* of those hypotheses which have not
stood up to them, and which are therefore rejected. It is important
to realize the consequences of this view. They are these: all tests
can be interpreted as attempts to weed out false theories—to find
the weak points of a theory in order to reject it if it is falsified by
the test. This view is sometimes considered paradoxical; our aim, it
is said, is to establish theories, not to eliminate false ones. But
just because it is our aim to establish theories as well as we can, we
must test them as severely as we can; that is, we must try to find fault
with them, we must try to falsify them. Only if we cannot falsify
them in spite of our best efforts can we say that they have stood
up to severe tests. This is the reason why the discovery of instances
which confirm a theory means very little if we have not tried, and
failed, to discover refutations. For if we are uncritical we shall always find what we want: we shall look for, and find, confirmations,
and we shall look away from, and not see, whatever might be
dangerous to our pet theories. In this way it is only too easy to
obtain what appears to be overwhelming evidence in favour of a
theory which, if approached critically, would have been refuted. In
order to make the method of selection by elimination work, and
to ensure that only the fittest theories survive, their struggle for life
must be made severe for them.

This, in outline, is the method of all sciences which are backed
by experience. But what about the method by which we *obtain*
our theories or hypotheses? What about *inductive generalizations,*

and the way in which we proceed from observation to theory? To
this question . . . I shall give two answers. (*a*) I do not believe
that we ever make inductive generalizations in the sense that we
start with observations and try to derive our theories from them. I
believe that the prejudice that we proceed in this way is a kind of
optical illusion, and that at no stage of scientific development do
we begin without something in the nature of a theory, such as a
hypothesis, or a prejudice, or a problem—often a technological
one—which in some way *guides* our observations, and helps us to
select from the innumerable objects of observation those which
may be of interest. But if this is so, then the method of elimination—
which is nothing but that of trial and error discussed [elsewhere]
—can always be applied. However, I do not think that it is necessary
for our present discussion to insist upon this point. For we can
say (*b*) that it is irrelevant from the point of view of science whether
we have obtained our theories by jumping to unwarranted conclusions or merely by stumbling over them (that is, by 'intuition'),
or else by some inductive procedure. The question, 'How did you
first *find* your theory?' relates, as it were, to an entirely private
matter, as opposed to the question, 'How did you *test* your theory?'
which alone is scientifically relevant. And the method of testing
described here is fertile; it leads to new observations, and to a
mutual give and take between theory and observation.

Now all this, I believe, is not only true for the natural but also
for the social sciences. And in the social sciences it is even more
obvious than in the natural sciences that we cannot see and observe
our objects before we have thought about them. For most of the
objects of social science, if not all of them, are abstract objects;
they are *theoretical* constructions. (Even 'the war' or 'the army' are
abstract concepts, strange as this may sound to some. What is concrete is the many who are killed; or the men and women in uniform,
etc.) These objects, these theoretical constructions used to interpret
our experience, are the result of constructing certain *models* (especially of institutions), in order to explain certain experiences—a
familiar theoretical method in the natural sciences (where we construct our models of atoms, molecules, solids, liquids, etc.). It is
part of the method of explanation by way of reduction, or deduction
from hypotheses. Very often we are unaware of the fact that we
are operating with hypotheses or theories, and we therefore mistake
our theoretical models for concrete things. This is a kind of mistake

which is only too common.[4] The fact that models are often used in this way explains—and by so doing destroys—the doctrines of methodological essentialism.[5] . . . It explains them, for the model is abstract or theoretical in character, and so we are liable to feel that we see it, either within or behind the changing observable events, as a kind of permanent ghost or essence. And it destroys them because the task of social theory is to construct and to analyse our sociological models carefully in descriptive or nominalist terms, that is to say, *in terms of individuals,* of their attitudes, expectations, relations, etc.—a postulate which may be called 'methodological individualism'.

The unity of the methods of the natural and social sciences may be illustrated and defended by an analysis of two passages from Professor Hayek's *Scientism and the Study of Society.*[6]

In the first of these passages, Professor Hayek writes:

'The physicist who wishes to understand the problems of the social sciences with the help of an analogy from his own field would have to imagine a world in which he knew by direct observation the inside of the atoms and had neither the possibility of making experiments with lumps of matter nor the opportunity to observe more than the interactions of a comparatively few atoms during a limited period. From his knowledge of the different kinds of atoms he could build up models of all the various ways in which they could combine into larger units and make these models more and more closely reproduce all the features of the few instances in which he was able to observe more complex phenomena. But the laws of the macrocosm which he could derive from his knowledge of the microcosm would always remain *"deductive"*; they would, because of his limited knowledge of the data of the complex situation, scarcely ever enable him to predict the precise outcome of a particular situation; and he could never verify them by controlled experiment—

[4] With this and the following paragraph, cp. F. A. von Hayek, 'Scientism and the Study of Society', parts I and II, *Economica*, vols. ix and x, where methodological collectivism is criticized and where methodological individualism is discussed in detail.

[5] In Section 10 of *The Poverty of Historicism*, Popper describes "methodological essentialism" as the position that the chief task of social science is to discover the "essences" of social entities and institutions in order to give definitive answers to questions such as "What is the State?", "What is a citizen?", "What is credit?".—Ed.

[6] For the two passages see *Economica*, vol. ix, p. 289 f. (italics mine).

although they might be *disproved* by the observation of events which according to his theory are impossible.'

I admit that the first sentence of this passage points to certain differences between social and physical science. But the rest of the passage, I believe, speaks for a complete *unity of method*. For if, as I do not doubt, this is a correct description of the method of social science, then it shows that it differs only from such interpretations of the method of natural science as we have already rejected. I have in mind, more especially, the 'inductivist' interpretation which holds that in the natural sciences we proceed systematically from observation to theory by some method of generalization, and that we can 'verify', or perhaps even prove, our theories by some method of induction. I have been advocating a very different view here—an interpretation of scientific method as deductive, hypothetical, selective by way of falsification, etc. And this description of the method of natural science agrees perfectly with Professor Hayek's description of the method of social science. (I have every reason to believe that my interpretation of the methods of science was not influenced by any knowledge of the methods of the social sciences; for when I developed it first, I had only the natural sciences in mind,[7] and I knew next to nothing about the social sciences.)

But even the differences alluded to in the first sentence of the quotation are not so great as may appear at first sight. It is undoubtedly true that we have a more direct knowledge of the 'inside of the human atom' than we have of physical atoms; but this knowledge is intuitive. In other words, we certainly use our knowledge of ourselves in order to frame *hypotheses* about some other people, or about all people. But these hypotheses must be tested, they must be submitted to the method of selection by elimination. (Intuition prevents some people from even imagining that anybody could possibly dislike chocolate.) The physicist, it is true, is not helped by such direct observation when he frames his hypotheses about atoms; nevertheless, he quite often uses some kind of sympathetic imagination or intuition which may easily make him feel that he is intimately acquainted with even the 'inside of the atoms' —with even their whims and prejudices. But this intuition is his private affair. Science is interested only in the hypotheses which

---

[7] Cp. *Erkenntnis*, III, p. 426 f., and my *Logik der Forschung* [The Logic of Scientific Discovery], 1934, whose sub-title may be translated: 'On the Epistemology of the Natural Sciences'.

his intuitions may have inspired, and then only if these are rich in consequences, and if they can be properly tested. . . .

In the second passage, Professor Hayek, speaking of social phenomena, says: '. . . our knowledge of the principle by which these phenomena are produced will rarely if ever enable us to predict the precise result of any *concrete* situation. While we can explain the principle on which certain phenomena are produced and can from this knowledge *exclude the possibility of certain results*, e.g. of certain events occurring together, our knowledge will in a sense be only negative, i.e. it will merely enable us to preclude certain results but not enable us to narrow the range of possibilities sufficiently so that only one remains'.

This passage, far from describing a situation peculiar to the social sciences, perfectly describes the character of natural laws which, indeed, can never do more than *exclude certain possibilities*. ('You cannot carry water in a sieve': see [below, p. 101].) More especially the statement that we shall not, as a rule, be able 'to predict the precise result of any *concrete* situation' opens up the problem of the inexactitude of prediction. . . . I contend that precisely the same may be said of the concrete physical world. In general it is only by the use of artificial experimental isolation that we can predict physical events. (The solar system is an exceptional case—one of natural, not of artificial isolation; once its isolation is destroyed by the intrusion of a foreign body of sufficient size, all our forecasts are liable to break down.) We are very far from being able to predict, even in physics, the precise results of a *concrete* situation, such as a thunderstorm, or a fire.

A very brief remark may be added here on the problem of complexity. . . . There is no doubt that the analysis of any concrete social situation is made extremely difficult by its complexity. But the same holds for any concrete physical situation.[8] The widely held prejudice that social situations are more complex than physical ones seems to arise from two sources. One of them is that we are liable to compare what should not be compared; I mean on the one hand concrete social situations and on the other hand artificially insulated experimental physical situations. (The latter might be compared, rather, with an artificially insulated social situation—such as a prison, or an experimental community.) The other source is the old

[8] A somewhat similar argument can be found in C. Menger, *Collected Works*, vol. II (1883 and 1933), pp. 259–60.

belief that the description of a social situation should involve the mental and perhaps even physical states of everybody concerned (or perhaps that it should even be reducible to them). But this belief is not justified; it is much less justified even than the impossible demand that the description of a concrete chemical reaction should involve that of the atomic and sub-atomic states of all the elementary particles involved (although chemistry may indeed be reducible to physics). The belief also shows traces of the popular view that social entities such as institutions or associations are concrete natural entities such as crowds of men, rather than abstract models constructed to interpret certain selected abstract relations between individuals.

But in fact, there are good reasons, not only for the belief that social science is less complicated than physics, but also for the belief that concrete social situations are in general less complicated than concrete physical situations. For in most social situations, if not in all, there is an element of *rationality*. Admittedly, human beings hardly ever act quite rationally (i.e. as they would if they could make the optimal use of all available information for the attainment of whatever ends they may have), but they act, none the less, more or less rationally; and this makes it possible to construct comparatively simple models of their actions and inter-actions, and to use these models as approximations.

The last point seems to me, indeed, to indicate a considerable difference between the natural and the social sciences—perhaps *the most important difference in their methods,* since the other important differences, i.e. specific difficulties in conducting experiments . . . and in applying quantitative methods (see below), are differences of degree rather than of kind. I refer to the possibility of adopting, in the social sciences, what may be called the method of logical or rational construction, or perhaps the 'zero method'.[9] By this I mean the method of constructing a model on the assumption of complete rationality (and perhaps also on the assumption of the possession of complete information) on the part of all the individuals concerned, and of estimating the deviation of the actual behaviour of people from the model behaviour, using the latter as a

[9] See the 'null hypothesis' discussed in J. Marschak, 'Money Illusion and Demand Analysis', in *The Review of Economic Statistics,* vol. XXV, p. 40.— The method described here seems partly to coincide with what has been called by Professor Hayek, following C. Menger, the 'compositive' method.

kind of zero co-ordinate.[10] An example of this method is the comparison between actual behaviour (under the influence of, say, traditional prejudice, etc.) and model behaviour to be expected on the basis of the 'pure logic of choice', as described by the equations of economics. . . .

In concluding this [discussion], I have to mention what I consider to be the other main difference between the methods of some of the theoretical sciences of nature and of society. I mean the specific difficulties connected with the application of quantitative methods, and especially methods of measurement.[11] Some of these difficulties can be, and have been, overcome by the application of statistical methods, for example in demand analysis. And they *have to be overcome* if, for example, some of the equations of mathematical economics are to provide a basis even of merely qualitative applications; for without such measurement we should often not know whether or not some counteracting influences exceeded an effect calculated in merely qualitative terms. Thus merely qualitative considerations may well be deceptive at times; just as deceptive, to quote Professor Frisch, 'as to say that when a man tries to row a boat forward, the boat will be driven backward because of the pressure exerted by his feet.' [12] But it cannot be doubted that there are some fundamental difficulties here. In physics, for example, the parameters of our equations can, in principle, be reduced to a small number of natural constants—a reduction which has been successfully carried out in many important cases. This is not so in economics; here the parameters are themselves in the most important cases quickly changing variables.[13] This clearly reduces the significance, interpretability, and testability of our measurements.

[10] Even here it may be said, perhaps, that the use of rational or 'logical' models in the social sciences, or of the 'zero method', has some vague parallel in the natural sciences, especially in thermodynamics and in biology (the construction of mechanical models, and of physiological models of processes and of organs). (Cp. also the use of variational methods.)

[11] These difficulties are discussed by Professor Hayek, *op. cit.*, p. 290 f.

[12] See *Econometrica*, I (1933), p. 1 f.

[13] See Lionel Robbins, in *Economica*, vol. V, especially p. 351.

B. F. SKINNER

# The Scheme of Behavior Explanations

*People who agree that the social sciences can use the hypothetical-deductive method with chances at least comparable to those of the natural sciences of triumphing over the objections hitherto discussed might differ among themselves about more specific conceptions of method. In the following selection, Skinner risks—perhaps, indeed, deliberately provokes—controversy by insisting that the study of human activities concentrate on forms of external behavior, exhibited with various frequencies and probabilities. In Skinner's late and relatively sophisticated version of behaviorism, organisms—including human beings—are assumed to have a capacity for initiatives of limited kinds. The organism moves first, as it were, and then conditioning takes place. But Skinner himself believes that scientific study on his approach, though it recognizes differences in intelligence, challenges traditional beliefs in the possibility of free choices. In one of the articles collected in his lively and diversified* Cumulative Record *(New York: Appleton-Century-Crofts, 1959) he says (p. 236) that a properly scientific theory of human behavior "must abolish the conception of the individual as a doer, as an originator of action," wholly renouncing the conception of inner psychic causes and "the inner man."*

## THE VARIABLES OF WHICH BEHAVIOR IS A FUNCTION

The practice of looking inside the organism for an explanation of behavior has tended to obscure the variables which are immediately available for a scientific analysis. These variables lie outside the organism, in its immediate environment and in its environmental history. They have a physical status to which the usual techniques of science are adapted, and they make it possible to explain behavior as other subjects are explained in science. These independent variables are of many sorts and their relations to behavior are often subtle and complex, but we cannot hope to give an adequate account of behavior without analyzing them.

Consider the act of drinking a glass of water. This is not likely to be an important bit of behavior in anyone's life, but it supplies a convenient example. We may describe the topography of the behavior in such a way that a given instance may be identified quite accurately by any qualified observer. Suppose now we bring someone into a room and place a glass of water before him. Will he drink? There appear to be only two possibilities: either he will or he will not. But we speak of the *chances* that he will drink, and this notion may be refined for scientific use. What we want to evaluate is the *probability* that he will drink. This may range from virtual certainty that drinking will occur to virtual certainty that it will not. The very considerable problem of how to measure such a probability will be discussed later. For the moment, we are interested in how the probability may be increased or decreased.

Everyday experience suggests several possibilities, and laboratory and clinical observations have added others. It is decidedly not true that a horse may be led to water but cannot be made to drink. By arranging a history of severe deprivation we could be "absolutely sure" that drinking would occur. In the same way we may be sure that the glass of water in our experiment will be drunk. Although we are not likely to arrange them experimentally, deprivations of the necessary magnitude sometimes occur outside the laboratory. We may obtain an effect similar to that of deprivation by speeding up the excretion of water. For example, we may induce sweating by raising the temperature of the room or by forcing heavy exercise, or we may increase the excretion of urine by mixing salt or urea in food taken prior to the experiment. It is also well known that loss of blood, as on a battlefield, sharply increases the probability of drinking. On the other hand, we may set the probability at virtually zero by inducing or forcing our subject to drink a large quantity of water before the experiment.

If we are to predict whether or not our subject will drink, we must know as much as possible about these variables. If we are to induce him to drink, we must be able to manipulate them. In both cases, moreover, either for accurate prediction or control, we must investigate the effect of each variable quantitatively with the methods and techniques of a laboratory science.

Other variables may, of course, affect the result. Our subject may be "afraid" that something has been added to the water as a practical joke or for experimental purposes. He may even "suspect" that the water has been poisoned. He may have grown up in a culture in which water is drunk only when no one is watching. He may refuse to drink simply to prove that we cannot predict or control his behavior. These possibilities do not disprove the relations between drinking and the variables listed in the preceding paragraphs; they simply remind us that other variables may have to be taken into account. We must know the history of our subject with respect to the behavior of drinking water, and if we cannot eliminate social factors from the situation, then we must know the history of his personal relations to people resembling the experimenter. Adequate prediction in any science requires information about all relevant variables, and the control of a subject matter for practical purposes makes the same demands.

Other types of "explanation" do not permit us to dispense with these requirements or to fulfill them in any easier way. It is of no help to be told that our subject will drink provided he was born under a particular sign of the zodiac which shows a preoccupation with water or provided he is the lean and thirsty type or was, in short, "born thirsty." Explanations in terms of inner states or agents, however, may require some further comment. To what extent is it helpful to be told, "He drinks because he is thirsty"? If to be thirsty means nothing more than to have a tendency to drink, this is mere redundancy. If it means that he drinks because of a state of thirst, an inner causal event is invoked. If this state is purely inferential— if no dimensions are assigned to it which would make direct observation possible—it cannot serve as an explanation. But if it has physiological or psychic properties, what role can it play in a science of behavior?

The physiologist may point out that several ways of raising the probability of drinking have a common effect: they increase the concentration of solutions in the body. Through some mechanism not yet well understood, this may bring about a corresponding change in the nervous system which in turn makes drinking more probable. In the same way, it may be argued that all these operations make the organism "feel thirsty" or "want a drink" and that such a psychic state also acts upon the nervous system in some unexplained way to induce drinking. In each case we have a causal chain consisting of three links: (1) an operation performed upon the organism from without—for example, water deprivation; (2) an inner condition—for example, physiological or psychic thirst; and (3) a kind of behavior —for example, drinking. Independent information about the second link would obviously permit us to predict the third without recourse to the first. It would be a preferred type of variable because it would be nonhistoric; the first link may lie in the past history of the organism, but the second is a current condition. Direct information about the second link is, however, seldom, if ever, available. Sometimes we infer the second link from the third: an animal is judged to be thirsty if it drinks. In that case, the explanation is spurious. Sometimes we infer the second link from the first: an animal is said to be thirsty if it has not drunk for a long time. In that case, we obviously cannot dispense with the prior history.

The second link is useless in the *control* of behavior unless we can manipulate it. At the moment, we have no way of directly altering neural processes at appropriate moments in the life of a behaving organism, nor has any way been discovered to alter a psychic process. We usually set up the second link through the first: we make an animal thirsty, in either the physiological or the psychic sense, by depriving it of water, feeding it salt, and so on. In that case, the second link obviously does not permit us to dispense with the first. Even if some new technical discovery were to enable us to set up or change the second link directly, we should still have to deal with those enormous areas in which human behavior is controlled through manipulation of the first link. A technique of operating upon the second link would increase our control of behavior, but the techniques which have already been developed would still remain to be analyzed.

The most objectionable practice is to follow the causal sequence back only as far as a hypothetical second link. This is a serious handicap both in a theoretical science and in the practical control of behavior. It is no help to be told that to get an organism to drink we are simply to "make it thirsty" unless we are also told how this is to be done. When we have obtained the necessary prescription for thirst, the whole proposal is more complex than it need be. Similarly, when an example of maladjusted behavior is explained by saying that the individual is "suffering from anxiety," we have still to be told the cause of the anxiety. But the external conditions which are then invoked could have been directly related to the maladjusted behavior. Again, when we are told that a man stole a loaf of bread because "he was hungry," we have still to learn of the external conditions responsible for the "hunger." These conditions would have sufficed to explain the theft.

The objection to inner states is not that they do not exist, but that they are not relevant in a functional analysis. We cannot account for the behavior of any system while staying wholly inside it; eventually we must turn to forces operating upon the organism from without. Unless there is a weak spot in our causal chain so that the second link is not lawfully determined by the first, or the third by the second, then the first and third links must be lawfully related. If we must always go back beyond the second link for prediction and control, we may avoid many tiresome and exhausting digressions by examining the third link as a function of the first. Valid information about the second link may throw light upon this relationship but can in no way alter it. . . .

## OPERANT CONDITIONING

. . . When we come to refine the notion of probability of response for scientific use, we find that . . . our data are frequencies and that the conditions under which they are observed must be specified. The main technical problem in designing a controlled experiment is to provide for the observation and interpretation of frequencies. We eliminate, or at least hold constant, any condition which encourages behavior which competes with the behavior we are to study. An organism is placed in a quiet box where its behavior may be observed through a one-way screen or recorded mechanically. This is by no means an environmental vacuum, for the organism will react to the features of the box in many ways; but its behavior will eventually reach a fairly stable level, against which the frequency of a selected response may be investigated. . . .

We select a relatively simple bit of behavior which may be freely and rapidly repeated, and which is easily observed and recorded. If our experimental subject is a pigeon, for example, the behavior of raising the head above a given height is convenient. This may be observed by sighting across the pigeon's head at a scale pinned on the far wall of the box. We first study the height at which the head is normally held and select some line on the scale which is reached only infrequently. Keeping our eye on the scale we then begin to open the food tray very quickly whenever the head rises above the line. If the experiment is conducted according to specifications, the result is invariable: we observe an immediate change in the frequency with which the head crosses the line. We also observe, and this is of some importance theoretically, that higher lines are now being crossed. We may advance almost immediately to a higher line in determining when food is to be presented. In a minute or two, the bird's posture has changed so that the top of the head seldom falls below the line which we first chose.

. . . We are reading something into our observations when we call any upward movement of the head a "trial," and there is no reason to call any movement which does not achieve a specified consequence an "error." Even the term "learning" is misleading. The statement that the bird "learns that it will get food by stretching its neck" is an inaccurate report of what has happened. To say that it has acquired the "habit" of stretching its neck is merely to resort to an explanatory fiction, since our only evidence of the habit is the acquired tendency to perform the act. The barest possible statement of the process is this: we make a given consequence contingent upon certain physical properties of behavior (the upward movement of the head), and the behavior is then observed to increase in frequency.

It is customary to refer to any movement of the organism as a "response." The word is borrowed from the field of reflex action and implies an act which, so to speak, answers a prior event—the stimulus. But we may make an event contingent upon behavior without identifying, or being able to identify, a prior stimulus. We did not alter the environment of the pigeon to *elicit* the upward movement of the head. It is probably impossible to show that any single stimulus invariably precedes this movement. Behavior of this sort may come under the control of stimuli, but the relation is not that of elicitation. The term "response" is therefore not wholly appropriate but is so well established that we shall use it in the following discussion.

A response which has already occurred cannot, of course, be predicted or controlled. We can only predict that *similar* responses will occur in the future. The unit of a predictive science is, therefore, not a response but a class of responses. The word "operant" will be used to describe this class. The term emphasizes the fact that the behavior *operates* upon the environment to generate consequences. The consequences define the properties with respect to which responses are called similar. The term will be used both as an adjective (operant behavior) and as a noun to designate the behavior defined by a given consequence.

A single instance in which a pigeon raises its head is a *response*. It is a bit of history which may be reported in any frame of reference we wish to use. The behavior called "raising the head," regardless of when specific instances occur, is an *operant*. . . .

. . . Pavlov . . . called all events which strengthened behavior "reinforcement" and all the resulting changes "conditioning." In the Pavlovian experiment, however, a reinforcer is paired with a *stimulus;* whereas in operant behavior it is contingent upon a *response*. Operant reinforcement is therefore a separate process and requires a separate analysis. In both cases, the strengthening of behavior which results from reinforcement is appropriately called "conditioning." In operant conditioning we "strengthen" an operant in the sense of making a response more probable or, in actual fact, more frequent. In Pavlovian or "respondent" conditioning we simply increase the magnitude of the response elicited by the conditioned stimulus and shorten the time which elapses between stimulus and response. (We note, incidentally; that these two cases exhaust the possibilities: an organism is conditioned when a reinforcer [1] accompanies another stimulus or [2] follows upon the organism's own behavior. Any event which does neither has no effect in changing a probability of response.) In the pigeon experiment, then, food is the *reinforcer* and presenting food when a response is emitted is the *reinforcement*. The *operant* is defined by the property upon which reinforcement is contingent—the height to which the head must be raised. The change in frequency with which the head is lifted to this height is the process of *operant conditioning*.

While we are awake, we act upon the environment constantly, and many of the consequences of our actions are reinforcing. Through operant conditioning the environment builds the basic repertoire with which we keep our balance, walk, play games, handle instruments and tools, talk, write, sail a boat, drive a car, or fly a plane. A change in the environment—a new car, a new friend, a new field of interest, a new job, a new location—may find us unprepared, but our behavior usually adjusts quickly as we acquire new responses and discard old. [Moreover,] operant reinforcement does more than build a behavioral repertoire. It improves the efficiency of behavior and maintains behavior in strength long after acquisition or efficiency has ceased to be of interest.

## QUANTITATIVE PROPERTIES

It is not easy to obtain a curve for operant conditioning. We cannot isolate an operant completely, nor can we eliminate all arbitrary details. In our example we might plot a curve showing how the frequency with which the pigeon's head is lifted to a given height changes with time or the number of reinforcements, but the total effect is clearly broader than this. There is a shift in a larger pattern of behavior, and to describe it fully we should have to follow all movements of the head. Even so, our account would not be complete. The height to which the head was to be lifted was chosen arbitrarily, and the effect of reinforcement depends upon this selection. If we reinforce a height which is seldom reached, the change in pattern will be far greater than if we had chosen a commoner height. For an adequate account we need a set of curves covering all the possibilities. Still another arbitrary element appears if we force the head to a higher and higher position, since we may follow different schedules in advancing the line selected for reinforcement. Each schedule will yield its own curve, and the picture would be complete only if it covered all possible schedules.

We cannot avoid these problems by selecting a response which is more sharply defined by features of the environment—for example, the behavior of operating a door latch. Some mechanical indicator of behavior is, of course, an advantage—for example, in helping us to reinforce consistently. We could record the height of a pigeon's head with a photocell arrangement, but it is simpler to select a response which makes a more easily recorded change in the environment. If the bird is conditioned to peck a small disk on the wall of the experimental box, we may use the movement of the disk to close an electric circuit—both to operate the food tray and to count or record responses. Such a response seems to be different from stretching the neck in that it has an all-or-none character. But . . . the mechanical features of striking a key do not define a "response" which is any less arbitrary than neck-stretching.

An experimental arrangement need not be perfect in order to provide important quantitative data in operant conditioning. We are already in a position to evaluate many factors. The importance of feed-back is clear. The organism must be stimulated by the consequences of its behavior if conditioning is to take place. In learning to wiggle one's ears, for example, it is necessary to know when the ears move if responses which produce movement are to be strengthened in comparison with responses which do not. In re-educating the patient in the use of a partially paralyzed limb, it may be of help to amplify the feed-back from slight movements, either with instruments or through the report of an instructor. The deaf-mute learns to talk only when he receives a feed-back from his own behavior which can be compared with the stimulation he receives from other speakers. One function of the educator is to supply arbitrary (sometimes spurious) consequences for the sake of feed-back. Conditioning depends also upon the kind, amount, and immediacy of reinforcement, as well as many other factors.

A single reinforcement may have a considerable effect. Under good conditions the frequency of a response shifts from a prevailing low value to a stable high value in a single abrupt step. More commonly we observe a substantial increase as the result of a single reinforcement, and additional increases from later reinforcements. The observation is not incompatible with the assumption of an instantaneous change to a maximal probability, since we have by no means isolated a single operant. The increased frequency must be interpreted with respect to other behavior characteristic of the situation. The fact that conditioning can be so rapid in an organism as "low" as the rat or pigeon has interesting implications. Differences in what is commonly called intelligence are attributed in part to differences in speed of learning. But there can be no faster learning than an instantaneous increase in probability of response. The superiority of human behavior is, therefore, of some other sort. . . .

## OPERANT EXTINCTION

When reinforcement is no longer forthcoming, a response becomes less and less frequent in what is called "operant extinction." If food is withheld, the pigeon will eventually stop lifting its head. In general when we engage in behavior which no longer "pays off," we find ourselves less inclined to behave in that way again. If we lose a fountain pen, we reach less and less often into the pocket which formerly held it. If we get no answer to telephone calls, we eventually stop telephoning. If our piano goes out of tune, we gradually play it less and less. If our radio becomes noisy or if programs become worse, we stop listening.

Since operant extinction takes place much more slowly than operant conditioning, the process may be followed more easily. Under suitable conditions smooth curves are obtained in which the rate of response is seen to decline slowly, perhaps over a period of many hours. The curves reveal properties which could not possibly be observed through casual inspection. We may "get the impression" that an organism is responding less and less often, but the orderliness of the change can be seen only when the behavior is recorded. The curves suggest that there is a fairly uniform process which determines the output of behavior during extinction. . . .

Behavior during extinction is the result of the conditioning which has preceded it, and in this sense the extinction curve gives an additional measure of the effect of reinforcement. If only a few responses have been reinforced, extinction occurs quickly. A long history of reinforcement is followed by protracted responding. The resistance to extinction cannot be predicted from the probability of response observed at any given moment. We must know the history of reinforcement. For example, though we have been reinforced with an excellent meal in a new restaurant, a bad meal may reduce our patronage to zero; but if we have found excellent food in a restaurant for many years, several poor meals must be eaten there, other things being equal, before we lose the inclination to patronize it again.

There is no simple relation between the number of responses reinforced and the number which appear in extinction. . . . The resistance to extinction generated by *intermittent* reinforcement may be much greater than if the same number of reinforcements are given for consecutive responses. Thus if we only occasionally reinforce a child for good behavior, the behavior survives after we discontinue reinforcement much longer than if we had reinforced every instance up to the same total number of reinforcements. This is of practical importance where the available reinforcers are limited. Problems of this sort arise in education, industry, economics, and many other fields. Under some schedules of intermittent reinforcement as many as 10,000 responses may appear in the behavior of a pigeon before extinction is substantially complete. . . .

### [CONDITIONING AND EVOLUTION]

In certain respects operant reinforcement resembles the natural selection of evolutionary theory. Just as genetic characteristics which arise as mutations are selected or discarded by their consequences, so novel forms of behavior are selected or discarded through reinforcement. . . .

. . . In both operant conditioning and the evolutionary selection of behavioral characteristics, consequences alter future probability. Reflexes and other innate patterns of behavior evolve because they increase the chances of survival of the *species*. Operants grow strong because they are followed by important consequences in the life of the *individual*. Both processes raise the question of purpose for the same reason, and in both the appeal to a final cause may be rejected in the same way. A spider does not possess the elaborate behavioral repertoire with which it constructs a web because that web will enable it to capture the food it needs to survive. It possesses this behavior because similar behavior on the part of spiders in the past has enabled *them* to capture the food *they* needed to survive. A series of events have been relevant to the behavior of web-making in its earlier evolutionary history. We are wrong in saying that we observe the purpose of the web when we observe similar events in the life of the individual.

ALFRED SCHUTZ

# The Social World and the
# Theory of Social Action

*Skinner insists as emphatically as he can on the "outside" point of view.
His emphasis will not go unchallenged. Schutz, in the following article—
which is the main turning point in the dialectic of this book—takes up the
"inside" point of view touched upon by Allport and Popper and argues
that this is the basic key to understanding human activities. Yet it will be
noted that subjective "understanding" (German, Verstehen) develops,
according to Schutz, an objectivity of its own. The motives with which
people interact with one another are generally interpreted by them as
typical motives, sometimes of typical actors—motives, one might suggest,
that are ascribed on the basis of publicly shared knowledge. In the end,
moreover, the social scientist who begins with the inside or subjective
point of view of ordinary life finds himself dealing with theoretically constructed "ideal types" of actors, whose systematically simplified motives
and actions are designed to represent objectively identifiable aspects of
social phenomena.*

*Alfred Schutz (1899–1959), like Popper, was born and educated in
Vienna. Unlike Popper, he was later much influenced by study with
Edmund Husserl (1859–1938), the founder of phenomenology. From
1943 to his death, Schutz was professor of philosophy and sociology at
the Graduate Faculty of the New School for Social Research in New York.*

At first sight it is not easily understandable why the subjective
point of view should be preferred in the social sciences. Why address
ourselves always to this mysterious and not too interesting tyrant of
the social sciences, called the subjectivity of the actor? Why not
honestly describe in honestly objective terms what really happens,
and that means speaking our own language, the language of qualified and scientifically trained observers of the social world? And if
it be objected that these terms are but artificial conventions created
by our "will and pleasure," and that therefore we cannot utilize

From Alfred Schutz, "The Social World and the Theory of Social Action,"
*Social Research: An International Quarterly of Political and Social Science,*
**XXVII** (Summer 1960), pp. 203–221. Copyright 1960 by *Social Research* and
reprinted by permission of the editors. [The article was edited for publication
after Schutz's death.]

them for real insight into the meaning which social acts have for those who act, but only for our interpretation, we could answer that it is precisely this building up of a system of conventions and an honest description of the world which *is* and is alone the task of scientific thought; that we scientists are no less sovereign in our system of interpretation than the actor is free in setting up his system of goals and plans; that we social scientists in particular have but to follow the pattern of natural sciences, which have performed with the very methods we should abandon the most wonderful work of all time; and, finally, that it is the essence of science to be objective, valid not only for me, or for me and you and a few others, but for everyone, and that scientific propositions do not refer to my private world but to the one and unitary life-world common to us all.

The last part of this thesis is incontestably true; but doubtless even a fundamental point of view can be imagined, according to which social sciences have to follow the pattern of natural sciences and to adopt their methods. Pushed to its logical conclusion it leads to the method of behaviorism. To criticize this principle is not within the scope of the present study. We restrict ourselves to the remark that radical behaviorism stands and falls with the basic assumption that there is no possibility of proving the intelligence of "the fellowman." It is highly probable that he is an intelligent human being, but that is a "weak fact" not capable of verification (Russell, similarly Carnap).

Yet, it is not then quite understandable why an intelligent individual should write books for others or even meet others in congresses where it is reciprocally proved that the intelligence of the other is a questionable fact. It is even less understandable that the same authors who are convinced that no verification is possible for the intelligence of other human beings have such confidence in the principle of verifiability itself, which can be realized only through cooperation with others by mutual control. Furthermore they feel no inhibition about starting all their deliberations with the dogma that language exists, that speech reactions and verbal reports are legitimate methods of behavioristic psychology, that propositions in a given language are able to make sense, without considering that language, speech, verbal report, proposition, and sense already presuppose intelligent alter egos, capable of understanding the language, of interpreting the proposition, and of verifying the sense.[1]

[1] John B. Watson, *Psychology, from the Standpoint of a Behaviorist*, 3rd ed. (Philadelphia: Lippincott, 1929) pp. 38 ff.

But the phenomena of understanding and interpreting themselves cannot be explained as pure behavior, provided we do not recur to the subterfuge of a "covert behavior" which evades a description in behavioristic terms.[2]

These few critical remarks, however, do not hit the center of our problem. Behaviorism as well as every other objective scheme of reference in the social sciences has, of course, as its chief purpose, to explain with scientifically correct methods what really happens in the social world of our everyday life. It is, of course, neither the goal nor the meaning of any scientific theory to design and to describe a fictitious world having no reference whatsoever to our common sense experience and being therefore without any practical interest for us. The fathers of behaviorism had no other purpose than that of describing and explaining real human acts within a real human world. But the fallacy of this theory consists in the substitution of a fictional world for social reality by promulgating methodological principles as appropriate for the social sciences which, though proved true in other fields, prove a failure in the realm of intersubjectivity.

But behaviorism is only one form of objectivism in the social sciences, though the most radical one. The student of the social world does not find himself placed before the inexorable alternative either of accepting the strictest subjective point of view, and, therefore, of studying the motives and thoughts in the mind of the actor; or of restricting himself to the description of the overt behavior and of admitting the behavioristic tenet of the inaccessibility of the other's mind and even of the unverifiability of the other's intelligence. There is rather a basic attitude conceivable—and, in fact, several of the most successful social scientists have adopted it—which accepts naively the social world with all the alter egos and institutions in it as a meaningful universe, meaningful namely for the observer whose only scientific task consists in describing and explaining his and his co-observers' experiences of it.

To be sure, those scientists admit that phenomena like nation, government, market, price, religion, art, science refer to activities of other intelligent human beings for whom they constitute the world of their social life; they admit furthermore that alter egos have created this world by their activities and that they orient their

[2] The foregoing remarks are only partially true for the so-called behavioristic position of the great philosopher and sociologist G. H. Mead (*Mind, Self and Society* [Chicago: University of Chicago Press, 1934], for example, pp. 2 ff.).

further activities to its existence. Nevertheless, so they pretend, we are not obliged to go back to the subjective activities of those alter egos and to their correlates in their minds in order to give a description and explanation of the facts of this social world. Social scientists, they contend, may and should restrict themselves to telling what this world means to them, neglecting what it means to the actors within this social world. Let us collect the facts of this social world, as our scientific experience may present them in a reliable form, let us describe and analyze these facts, let us group them under pertinent categories and study the regularities in their shape and development which then will emerge, and we shall arrive at a system of the social sciences, discovering the basic principles and the analytical laws of the social world. Having once reached this point the social sciences may confidently leave the subjective analyses to psychologists, philosophers, metaphysicists, or however else you like to call idle people bothering with such problems. And, the defender of such a position may add, is it not this scientific ideal which the most advanced social sciences are about to realize? Look at modern economics! The great progress of this science dates exactly from the decision of some advanced spirits to study curves of demand and supply and to discuss equations of prices and costs instead of striving hard and in vain to penetrate the mystery of subjective wants and subjective values.

Doubtless such a position is not only possible but even accepted by the majority of social scientists. Doubtless on a certain level real scientific work may be performed and has been performed without entering into the problems of subjectivity. We can go far ahead in the study of social phenomena, like social institutions of all kinds, social relations, and even social groups, without leaving the basic frame of reference, which can be formulated as follows: what does all this mean for us, the scientific observer? We can develop and apply a refined system of abstraction for this purpose which intentionally eliminates the actor in the social world, with all his subjective points of view, and we can even do so without coming into conflict with the experiences derived from social reality. Masters in this technique—and there are many of them in all fields of social research—will always guard against leaving the consistent level within which this technique may be adopted and they will therefore confine their problems adequately.

All this does not alter the fact that this type of social science does not deal directly and immediately with the social life-world, common to us all, but with skillfully and expediently chosen idealizations and formalizations of the social world which are not repugnant to its facts. Nor does it make the less indispensable reference to the subjective point of view on other levels of abstraction if the original problem under consideration is modified. But then—and that is an important point—this reference to the subjective point of view always *can* be performed and should be performed. As the social world under any aspect whatsoever remains a very complicated cosmos of human activities, we can always go back to the "forgotten man" of the social sciences, to the actor in the social world whose doing and feeling lies at the bottom of the whole system. We, then, try to understand him in that doing and feeling and the state of mind which induced him to adopt specific attitudes towards his social environment.

In such a case the answer to the question "what does this social world mean for me the observer?" requires as a prerequisite the answering of the quite other questions "what does this social world mean for the observed actor within this world and what did he mean by his acting within it?" In putting our questions thus we no longer naively accept the social world and its current idealizations and formalizations as ready-made and meaningful beyond all question, but we undertake to study the process of idealizing and formalizing as such, the genesis of the meaning which social phenomena have for us as well as for the actors, the mechanism of the activity by which human beings understand one another and themselves. We are always free, and sometimes obliged, to do so. . . .

The scientific observer's decision to study the social world under an objective or subjective frame of reference circumscribes from the beginning the section of the social world (or, at least, the aspect of such a section) which is capable of being studied under the scheme chosen once and for all. The basic postulate of the methodology of social science, therefore, must be the following: choose the scheme of reference adequate to the problem you are interested in, consider its limits and possibilities, make its terms compatible and consistent with one another, and having once accepted it, stick to it! If, on the other hand, the ramifications of your problem lead you in the progress of your work to the acceptance of other schemes of reference and interpretation, do not forget that with the change in the scheme all terms in the formerly used scheme necessarily undergo a shift of

and this means I have to be able to interpret them as possible relevant elements for possible acts or reactions I might perform within the scope of my life plans.

But from the beginning this orientation through understanding occurs in cooperation with other human beings: this world has meaning not only for me but also for you and you and everyone. My experience of the world justifies and corrects itself by the experience of the others with whom I am interrelated by common knowledge, common work, and common suffering. The world, interpreted as the possible field of action for us all: that is the first and most primitive principle of organization of my knowledge of the exterior world in general. Afterwards I discriminate between natural things, which may be defined as things essentially given to me and you and everyone, such as they are, independent of any human interference, and on the other hand, social things, which are understandable only as products of human activity, my own or others' (the term "thing" used in both cases in its broadest sense, covering not only corporeal objects, but also "ideal"—mental—ones).

Concerning natural things my "understanding" is limited to the insight into their existence, variations, developments, in so far as all these elements are compatible with all my experiences and those of others within the natural world in general and with the basic assumptions about the structure of this world we all accept by common agreement. Within these limits prediction (though only of likelihood) is possible for us all. This thing here is, in my opinion and in the opinion of us all, a wild apple tree. This implies that it will bear blossoms in spring, leaves in summer, fruits in fall, and become bare in winter. If we want to have a better view, we may climb to its top; if we need relaxation in the summer, we may rest in its shade; if we are hungry in the fall, we may taste its fruits. All these possibilities are independent of any human agency; the cycle of natural events revolves without our interference.[3]

If I want to do so, there is no objection to calling this organized knowledge of natural facts an "understanding" of them. But used in this larger sense the term "understanding" means nothing else

---

[3] Of course the interpretation of natural things as products of the agency of another intelligence (though not a human one) is always an overt possibility. The life of the tree is then the result of the activities of a demon or of a dryad, etc.

than the reducibility of known and tested facts to other known and tested facts. If I consult an expert in the physiology of plants in order to learn what is really behind the afore-named cycle in vegetative life, he will refer me to the chemistry of chlorophyl or to the morphological structure of cells; in short he will "explain" the facts by reducing them to others, which have a greater generality and which have been tested in a broader field.

Quite another "understanding" is peculiar to social things (this term embracing also human acts). In this case it is not sufficient to refer the fact under consideration to other facts or things. I cannot understand a social thing without reducing it to the human activity which has created it and, beyond it, without referring this human activity to the motives out of which it springs. I do not understand a tool without knowing the purpose for which it was designed, a sign or a symbol without knowing what it stands for, an institution if I am unfamiliar with its goals, a work of art if I neglect the intentions of the artist which it realizes. . . .

The simplest complex of meaning in terms of which an action is interpreted by the actor are its motives. But this term is equivocal and covers two different categories which have to be well distinguished: the in-order-to motive and the because motive.[4] The former refers to the future and is identical with the object or purpose for the realization of which the action itself is a means: it is a "terminus ad quem." [5] The latter refers to the past and may be called its reason or cause: it is a "terminus a quo." Thus the action is determined by the project including the in-order-to motive. The project is the intended act imagined as already accomplished, the in-order-to motive is the future state of affairs to be realized by the projected action, and the project itself is determined by the because motive. The complexes of meaning which constitute the in-order-to motive and the because motive respectively differ from one another in that the first is an integral part of the action itself, whereas the latter requires a special act of reflection in the pluperfect tense, which will be carried out by the actor only if there are sufficient pragmatic reasons for him to do so.

[4] I borrow some English terms from the excellent study A. Stonier and Karl Bode published about my theory under the title "A New Approach to the Methodology of the Social Sciences," in *Economica* (November 1937) pp. 406–24.

[5] *Ad quem:* "to which"; *a quo:* "from which."—Ed.

It must be added that neither the claims of in-order-to motives nor the claims of because motives are chosen at random by the actor performing a concrete act. On the contrary, they are organized in great subjective systems. The in-order-to motives are integrated into subjective systems of planning: life plan, plans for work and leisure, plans for the "next time," time table for today, necessity of the hour, and so on. The because motives are grouped into systems which are treated in American [scientific] literature . . . correctly under the caption of (social) personality. The self's manifold experiences of its own basic attitudes in the past as they are condensed in the form of principles, maxims, habits, but also tastes, affects, and so on are the elements for building up the systems which can be personified. The latter is a very complicated problem requiring most earnest deliberation.

Above all, I cannot understand other people's acts without knowing the in-order-to or the because motives of such acts. To be sure, there are manifold degrees of understanding. I must not (even more, I cannot) grasp the full ramifications of other people's motives, with their horizons of individual life plans, their background of individual experiences, their references to the unique situation by which they are determined. As we said before, such an ideal understanding would presuppose the full identity of my stream of thought with that of the alter ego, and that would mean an identity of both our selves. It suffices, therefore, that I can reduce the other's act to its typical motives, including their reference to typical situations, typical ends, typical means, etc.

On the other hand, there are also different degrees of my knowledge of the actor himself, degrees of intimacy and anonymity. I may reduce the product of human activity to the agency of an alter ego with whom I share present time and present space, and then it may occur that this other individual is an intimate friend of mine or a passenger I meet for the first time and will never meet again. It is not necessary even that I know the actor personally in order to have an approach to his motives. I can for instance understand the acts of a foreign statesman and discuss his motives without having ever met him or even without having seen a picture of him. The same is true for individuals who have lived long before my own time; I can understand the acts and motives of Caesar as well as of the cave-man who left no other testimony of his existence than the firestone hatchet exhibited in the showcase of the museum. But it is not even necessary to reduce human acts to a more or less well known individual actor. To understand them it is sufficient to find typical motives of typical actors which explain the act as a typical one arising out of a typical situation. There is a certain conformity in the acts and motives of priests, soldiers, servants, farmers everywhere and at every time. Moreover, there are acts of such a general type that it is sufficient to reduce them to "somebody's" typical motives for making them understandable.

All this must be carefully investigated as an essential part of the theory of social action.[6] Summing up, we come to the conclusion that social things are only understandable if they can be reduced to human activities; and human activities are only made understandable by showing their in-order-to or because motives. The deeper reason for this fact is that as I naively live within the social world I am able to understand other people's acts only if I can imagine that I myself would perform analogous acts if I were in the same situation, directed by the same because motives, or oriented by the same in-order-to motives—all these terms understood in the restricted sense of the "typical" analogy, the "typical" sameness, as explained before.

That this assertion is true can be demonstrated by an analysis of the social action in the more precise sense of this term, namely of an action which involves the attitudes and actions of others and is oriented to them in its course.[7] As yet we have dealt in this study only with action as such without entering into the analysis of the modification which the general scheme undergoes with the introduction of social elements proper: mutual correlation and intersubjective adjustment. We have, therefore, observed the attitude of an isolated actor without making any distinction as to whether this actor is occupied with the handling of a tool or acting with others and for others, motivated by others and motivating them.

[6] An attempt was made by the present writer in his book *Der sinnhafte Aufbau der sozialen Welt* (Vienna, 1932; 2d ed. 1960).

[7] Max Weber, *Wirtschaft und Gesellschaft* (Tübingen 1922; new ed. 1956). Parts of this important work are available in English translation in H. H. Gerth and C. Wright Mills, eds., *From Max Weber: Essays in Sociology* (New York: Oxford University Press, 1946); other parts in the English translation by [A. M. Henderson and] Talcott Parsons, under the title *The Theory of Social and Economic Organization* (New York: Oxford University Press, 1947).

This topic is very complicated to analyze and we have to restrict ourselves to sketching its outlines. It can be proved that all social relations as they are understood by me, a human being living naively in the social world which is centered around myself, have their prototype in the social relation connecting myself with an individual alter ego with whom I am sharing space and time. My social act, then, is oriented not only to the physical existence of this alter ego but to the other's act which I expect to provoke by my own action. I can, therefore, say that the other's reaction is the in-order-to motive of my own act. The prototype of all social relationship is an intersubjective connection of motives. If I imagine, projecting my act, that you will understand my act and that this understanding will induce you to react, on your part, in a certain way, I anticipate that the in-order-to motives of my own acting will become because motives of your reaction, and vice-versa.

Let us take a very simple example. I ask you a question. The in-order-to motive of my act is not only the expectation that you will understand my question, but also to get your answer; or more precisely, I reckon *that* you will answer, leaving undecided what the content of your answer may be. *Modo futuri exacti* [8] I anticipate in projecting my own act that you will have answered my question in some way or other, and this means I think there is a fair chance that the understanding of my question will become a because motive for your answer, which I expect. The question, so we can say, is the because motive of the answer, as the answer is the in-order-to motive of the question. This interrelationship between my own and your motives is a well tested experience of mine, though, perhaps, I have never had explicit knowledge of the complicated interior mechanism of it. But I myself had felt on innumerable occasions induced to react to another's act, which I had interpreted as a question addressed to me, with a kind of behavior of which the in-order-to motive was my expectation that the other, the questioner, might interpret my behavior as an answer. Over against this experience I know that I have succeeded frequently in provoking another person's answer by my own act called questioning and so on. Therefore I feel I have a fair chance of getting your answer when I shall have once realized my action of questioning. . . .

[8] *Modo futuri exacti:* "in the future perfect tense."—Ed.

The social world in which I live as one connected with others through manifold relations is for me an object to be interpreted as meaningful. It makes sense to me, but by the same token I am sure it makes sense to others too. I suppose, furthermore, that my acts oriented to others will be understood by them in an analogous manner as I understand the acts of others oriented to me. More or less naively I presuppose the existence of a common scheme of reference for both my own acts and the acts of others. I am interested above all not in the overt behavior of others, not in their performance of gestures and bodily movements, but in their intentions, and that means in the in-order-to motives for the sake of which, and in the because motives based on which, they act as they do.

Convinced that they want to express something by their act or that their act has a specific position within the common frame of reference, I try to catch the meaning which the act in question has, particularly for my co-actors in the social world, and, until presented with counter-evidence, I presume that this meaning for them, the actors, corresponds to the meaning their act has for me. As I have to orient my own social acts to the because motives of the other's social acts oriented to me, I must always find out their in-order-to motives and disentangle the texture of social inter-relationship by interpreting other people's acts from the subjective point of view of the actor. That is the great difference between the attitude of a man who lives amidst manifold social interrelations in which he is interested as a party and the pure observer who is disinterested in the outcome of a social situation in which he does not participate and which he studies with a detached mind. . . .

But if the principle of safeguarding the subjective point of view in the social sciences were even admitted, how is it possible to deal scientifically—and that means in objective conceptual terms—with such subjective phenomena? The greatest difficulty lies, first of all, in the specific attitude the scientific observer has adopted towards the social world. As a scientist—not as a man among other men, which he is too—he is not a party in social interrelationship. He does not participate in the living stream of mutual testing of the in-order-to motives of his own acts by the reactions of others, and vice-versa. Strictly speaking, as a pure observer of the social world, the social scientist does not act. In so far as he "acts scientifically" (publishing papers, discussing problems with others, teaching) his activity is performed *within* the social world: he acts as man among other men, dealing with science, but he no longer has, then, the specific attitude of a scientific observer. This attitude is characterized by the fact that it is performed in complete aloofness. To become a social scientist the observer must make up his mind to step out of the social world, to drop any practical interest in it, and to restrict his in-order-to motives to the honest description and explanation of the social world which he observes.

But how should this job be performed? Not being able to communicate directly with the actors within the social world, he is unable to verify directly the data he has obtained about them from the different sources of information open to him within the social world. To be sure, he himself has, as a man among others, direct human experiences of the social world. In that capacity he can send out questionnaires, hear witnesses, establish test-cases. From these sources and others he gathers data which he will later use, once retired into the solitude of the theoretician. But his theoretical task as such begins with the building up of a conceptual scheme under which his information about the social world may be grouped.

It is one of the outstanding features of modern social science to have described the device the social scientists use in building up their conceptual scheme, and it is the great merit of [Durkheim, Pareto, Marshall, Veblen, and] above all of Max Weber, to have developed this technique in all its fullness and clarity. This technique consists in replacing the human beings which the social scientist observes as an actor on the social stage by puppets created by himself, in other words, in constructing ideal types of actors. This is done in the following way.

The scientist observes certain events within the social world as caused by human activity and he begins to establish a type of such events. Afterwards he coordinates with these typical acts typical because motives and in-order-to motives which he assumes as invariable in the mind of an imaginary actor. Thus he constructs a personal ideal type, which means the model of an actor whom he imagines as gifted with a consciousness. But it is a consciousness restricted in its content only to all those elements necessary for the performance of the typical acts under consideration. These elements it contains completely, but nothing beyond them. He imputes to it constant in-order-to motives corresponding to the goals which are realized within the social world by the acts under consideration; furthermore he ascribes to it constant because motives of such a structure that they may serve as a basis for the system of the presupposed constant in-order-to motives; finally he bestows on the ideal type such segments of life plans and such stocks of experiences as are necessary for the imaginary horizons and backgrounds of the puppet actor. The social scientist places these constructed types in a setting which contains all the elements of the situation in the social world relevant for the performance of the typical act under inquiry. Moreover, he associates with him other personal ideal types with motives apt to provoke typical reactions to the first ideal type's typical act.

So he arrives at a model of the social world, or better at a reconstruction of it. It contains all the relevant elements of the social event chosen as a typical one by the scientist for further examination. And it is a model which complies perfectly with the postulate of the subjective point of view. For from the first the puppet type is imagined as having the same specific knowledge of the situation—including means and conditions—which a real actor would have in the real social world; from the first the subjective motives of a real actor performing a typical act are implanted as constant elements of the specious consciousness of the personal ideal type; and it is the destiny of the personal ideal type to play the role the actor in the social world would have to adopt in order to perform the typical act. And as the type is constructed in such a way that it performs exclusively typical acts, the objective and subjective elements in the formation of unit-acts coincide.

On the other hand, the formation of the type, the choice of the typical event, and the elements considered as typical are conceptual terms which can be discussed objectively and which are open to criticism and verification. They are not formed by social scientists at random without check or restraint; the laws of their formation are very rigid and the scope of arbitrariness of the social scientist is much narrower than seems at first sight. We are unable to enter into this problem within this study. But briefly we will summarize what was brought out elsewhere.[9]

[9] I have sketched some of the principles ruling the formation of ideal types in a lecture delivered in the Faculty Club of Harvard University under the title "The Problem of Rationality in the Social World." (This lecture was published, under the same title, in *Economica*, May 1943—Eds., *Social Research*.)

1) *Postulate of relevance.* The formation of ideal types must comply with the principle of relevance, which means that the problem once chosen by the social scientist creates a scheme of reference and constitutes the limits of the scope within which relevant ideal types might be formed.

2) *Postulate of adequacy.* It may be formulated as follows: each term used in a scientific system referring to human action must be so constructed that a human act performed within the life world by an individual actor in the way indicated by the typical construction would be reasonable and understandable for the actor himself as well as for his fellowman.

3) *Postulate of logical consistency.* The system of ideal types must remain in full compatibility with the principles of formal logic.

4) *Postulate of compatibility.* The system of ideal types must contain only scientifically verifiable assumptions, which have to be fully compatible with the whole of our scientific knowledge.

These postulates give the necessary guarantees that social sciences do in fact deal with the real social world, the one and unitary life-world of us all, and not with a strange fancy-world independent of and without connection to this everyday life-world. To go further into the details of the typifying method seems to me one of the most important tasks of a theory of action.

OMAR K. MOORE AND ALAN R. ANDERSON

# Puzzles, Games, and Social Interaction

*One way of expressing Schutz's point that actions can be understood as typical actions done for typical motives is to say that they can be explained as actions done for reasons which as a* rule *govern such actions. The concept of rules (or norms) has a peculiar importance for the argument that human actions are to be understood on a different basis from the behavior of organisms; for it may be held that organisms other than human do not, like humans, follow rules. But what exactly are rules and exactly what difference does following them make to human beings? Moore and Anderson tie up the somewhat elusive concept of rules with particular varieties of play-activity, and argue that the varieties of rules and of (self-conscious) rule-following found in puzzles and games illustrate—and engender—essential aspects of social interaction and of socially-formed personalities.*

*Omar K. Moore (1920–    ), professor of psychology at Rutgers, has made notable experimental studies of the sociology of small groups and of the learning capacities of very young children. Alan R. Anderson (1925–    ), professor of philosophy at the University of Pittsburgh, is a logician who has been especially interested in the sociological applications of modal and deontic logic. He and Moore have collaborated in many studies of sociological theory and of the logic of norms.*

Theories of games of chance ("probability theory") and theories of games of strategy (after von Neumann) . . . grew directly out of the study of *autotelic* activities—that is, activities undertaken by human beings solely because of their intrinsic interest. Engaging in social games, playing with puzzles or aesthetic objects, simply being sociable, are examples of activities we call *autotelic*, i.e., activities which are, or should be, undertaken solely because they are enjoyable.

The close connection between game theory and probability theory on the one hand, and social games on the other, is not open

From Omar K. Moore and Alan R. Anderson, "Some Puzzling Aspects of Social Interaction," *The Review of Metaphysics*, **XV** (March 1962), pp. 410–412, 413–416, 424–425; "The Structure of Personality," *ibid.*, **XVI** (December 1962), pp. 223–226, 227–230, 230–231. Copyright 1962 by *The Review of Metaphysics*. Reprinted by permission of the editors of the *Review* and the authors.

to question. It is simply a fact of history that for both theories, the first models to be considered were ordinary social games. But one may wish to raise doubts about the claim that social games and the like are *autotelic* (especially if one belongs to one of the more austere schools of social psychology according to which it is not possible for *anyone* ever to do *anything* just for fun). To such critics we make the following minor concession (perhaps putting the matter in a way which will satisfy even the most puritanical): even if no one ever does enjoy anything, the rules of our society make it clear that people are under an *obligation* to enjoy *some* things, at least. There are severely sanctioned rules, for example, to the effect that one should take part in sports only because one wants to play. We are all supposed to give short shrift to grand-standers, cheaters, and people who "let the side down" or otherwise exhibit "bad form." And the rules governing autotelic activity, which have the effect of *keeping* the activity autotelic, are remarkably pervasive. We may not do business at a party; we may not go to the opera in order to be seen there by the right people; we may not join the country club simply to meet the right people. Rather: we must go to the party because we enjoy being sociable; we must go to the opera because we love music; we must join the country club because we like golf. People break these rules, of course; but it seems clear that there *are* such rules to be broken, and also that *some* behavior is autotelic in the required sense (i.e., that *sometimes* these rules are consciously complied with).

Now the striking fact that both these mathematical theories, probability theory and game theory, have models not only in the autotelic activities which led to their development, but also in the successful conduct of the more serious matters of survival and welfare, suggests the possibility that in acting autotelically we are "modeling" our own more serious behavior. This idea seems to be at the bottom of "formal sociology," in the sense of Simmel,[1] who talks, for example, about sociability as the "play form" of sociation: at a party we engage playfully in competition, coöperation, deceit, love, hostility, and the thousand and one other forms that social behavior may take—but we *play* at it, for no stakes.

[These considerations can be summed up] as follows: It might prove fruitful to look at autotelic cultural products (puzzles, games

[1] Simmel, G., *The Sociology of Georg Simmel,* Glencoe, Ill.: Free Press, 1950.

of chance, games of strategy, plays, novels, and the like) as *models* in the folk-culture, or *folk-models*, of the serious concerns of survival and human welfare—models with the help of which we come to understand and "be at home with" our natural and social environments. So put the thesis risks banality; what gives the thesis such teeth as it has, is the fact that social games and certain serious (say) economic problems are models of the same theory (regardless of the actual behavior of players, buyers, and sellers), and so may be said to have a *formal* similarity sufficient to lend some credibility to our contention. . . .

It is characteristic of social interaction that I cannot maximize my own utility without "taking into account" (in some vague sense which we understand only darkly) what *you* are up to. I must have some theories or intuitions about how you are likely to behave, how you will respond to my actions, and the like. Worse than that, I must be aware that you are very likely doing the same thing in regard to me, and I have to take *that* possibility into account as well. But of course you may know that I am aware of this possibility, and you adjust your behavior accordingly. And so it goes—we are both involved in a tortuous labyrinth of relations, and though we act in this way quite easily and freely, it is better than even money that neither of us could even *begin* to give an explicit account of how we do it. (It is the complexity of this kind of behavior, together with our inability to explain it, which lends plausibility to the suggestion that we *learn* to behave in this way by playing games of strategy. This is *exactly* the kind of behavior hide-and-seek (say) requires—but in hide-and-seek, failure to win is relatively inexpensive.)

The interactional models provided by games of strategy may be contrasted with the noninteractional models found in puzzles. It is of course true that we *can* regard puzzles as one-player games —but it still seems clear that puzzles do not share the interactional features of games of strategy. Once the conditions of a puzzle are set, they do not change on us suddenly with a view to thwarting our efforts at a solution; indeed this is exactly how we distinguish between "puzzles" and "games": no social interaction takes place between the puzzle and the solver.

Now if we are correct in our estimate of the importance of such folk-models as puzzles and games of strategy for the process which sociologists call "socialization," we should expect that their influence would be pervasive, and that their presence in the backs of our minds might, in subtle ways, not only intervene in much of our thinking, but even constitute the warp and woof of many of our thought patterns. Acting on this assumption, at any rate, we shall now try to develop some plausible considerations concerning the relations between these folk-models and scientific inquiry.

We observe first that both natural and behavioral sciences are, among other things, social enterprises, undertaken in a societal context, and that they both presuppose social selves (in the sense of Mead),[2] capable of social *interaction*. Now our own informal observations lead us to believe that the principal problems faced by (and produced by) infants, at least as they begin to learn speech, are interactional in character: the problems faced have to do with certain social rules, as laid down, enforced by, or exemplified by, other human beings. There are many examples: talking in accord with linguistic conventions, eating, toilet-training, playing together peaceably, respecting seniors, etc. All of these activities are rule-ridden,[3] and it seems plausible to suggest therefore that social games should be prior, both temporally and in order of importance, to puzzles, in the socialization process. Even non-interactional folk-models, say puzzles, presuppose social interaction, in the sense that they require a social context, and an ability to understand the restraints put on those artificial problems we call "puzzles."

Indeed we find some support for the notion that interactional models have a deep hold on us from the prevalence of animistic thinking in so-called "primitive" societies. In fact it is hard to eradicate even in "civilized" societies; many research scientists half-believe Finagle's Laws (which presuppose that inanimate objects are out to get us).

In social interaction we recognize that our opposite number is potentially friendly, potentially hostile, potentially indifferent, to us and our concerns. It would moreover seem quite natural, especially in a state of ignorance, to endow nature with these same

---

[2] Mead, G. H., *Mind, Self, and Society*, Chicago: University [of Chicago] Press, 1934.

[3] The importance of the concept *following a rule*, especially a linguistic rule, has probably been recognized more clearly by Wittgenstein [in *Philosophical Investigations*, New York: The Macmillan Co., 1953] than by anyone else in the history of philosophy, sociology, or psychology.

attributes. This is in fact a sound conservative strategy and one we have all followed from time to time. A person finding an inert bat on his doorstep does well to treat it as if it were alive until he is pretty certain that it is not. If we know little of nature generally, it might do trivial harm, and considerable good, if we treat nature as if it *might*, suddenly, turn on us.[4]

Now it seems to us to require a vertiginous act of abstraction to *remove* the interactional elements from our view of nature. "Dehumanizing" an anthropomorphic nature ought to require a sizable wrench, as experience with civilizing primitive peoples indicates. It is therefore not altogether surprising that it took millennia of human history before the natural sciences developed, especially if it is conceded that physics demands an abandonment of animism. It is central to the classical Newtonian view of natural phenomena that they be regarded as isolated systems, which run entirely by themselves, and are not influenced at all by *us*. Nature is, in short, assimilated to a puzzle.[5] *People* (as opposed to *bodies*) have been eradicated from the picture as ruthlessly and as completely as may be, and we are left with a mindless mechanism which dominated, and still dominates, the attitude of many working natural scientists. No one of course can maintain that as a heuristic principle, mechanism has been unsuccessful in the natural sciences—our

---

[4] We note that this fiction of a hostile, animistic nature lies behind Wald's treatment [in *Statistical Decision Functions*, New York: John Wiley & Sons, 1950] of confidence levels in the behavioral sciences. For a similar idea see Moore [O. K., "Divination—a New Perspective," *American Anthropologist*, February 1957, pp. 69–74].

[5] It might be objected that a conception of natural processes devoid of social interaction was known to several early Greek cosmologists, for example Democritus, and that consequently we are on shaky ground historically. In reply we explain that we do not mean to hold the position in such a sharp form. It must at least be conceded that Homer and Hesiod had a view of nature which was pervaded by social interaction—and all we wish to claim is that the latter kind of view is likely to come first. Even so, the classical views which pervaded western attempts at science up until the scientific Renaissance were those of Aristotle which, if not involving social interaction explicitly, at least embodied many anthropomorphic norms. Planets moved in circular orbits *because* (as Aristotle and his colleagues seemed to feel) circular motion was the *most perfect* form of nonrectilinear motion. And an early critic of Galileo's claim to have found an eighth planet cited in opposition the facts that there were seven deadly sins, seven cardinal virtues, seven days of the week, seven apertures in the head—*it stands to reason* that there are seven planets.

astonishing theoretical and technological progress would seem to indicate that this is *precisely* the right view to take, as regards physics.

In view of the success of the puzzle model in the natural sciences, it is not at all surprising that those interested in the behavioral sciences should have tried equally to remove *people* from their considerations. The principal thesis of behaviorism, at least in its early and crude forms, was that a human organism is a black box, subject to certain inputs and outputs, which should be studied like any other physical system. Social and psychological processes were to be regarded as isolated phenomena of a mechanistic sort, to be studied in complete abstraction from the social, inter-actional context in which they occur. Such an attitude is at least strongly suggested by the preoccupation in the first half of this century with rote-learning experiments and psycho-physical meas-urements, and more recently by attempts to simulate various kinds of problem-solving on computers. . . .

Consider the following problem. Suppose you were to find yourself on a lifeless moon, with no possibility of returning to, or communicating with, the earth. Suppose also that you were in a frame of mind to do something bad. What would you do?

In informal conversation, this question has elicited a wide variety of initial responses, but after a little thought the answer generally settles on the following point: the only way to do some-thing bad in those circumstances is somehow to break some *rule*. It may be moot whether there are any rules to break in the quasi-solipsistic universe we are considering; the examples we have heard (spitting, say, or offending God, or oneself, by committing suicide) have a farfetched ring to them. But note that even this kind of outrageous rule-breaking is doing something *against* some-one or something: the idea of rule-breaking in which no one (or nothing) gets hurt in any way seems, or seems almost, self-con-tradictory. . . .

We have, in this essay, been trying (from time to time) to appear to be sane arguers, and also (from time to time) to say what we believe, even without the kind of evidence we would like to have. Here we come on one of the latter points. The "conclusion" seems to us inescapable that *self-consciously acting in accordance with a rule* (or formulating such rule) is one of the fundamental aspects of social interaction, and any experimental studies which neglect this point simply have nothing to do with that topic. Indeed this is implicit in our earlier claims that social games of strategy are *models* of social interaction; obedience to game rules must be self-conscious. The whole point is, as Hume [6] says in comparing games with other social interaction:

> In societies for play, there are laws required for the conduct of the game; and these laws are different in each game. The foundation, I own, of such societies is frivolous; and the laws are, in a great measure, though not altogether, capricious and arbitrary. . . . The comparison, therefore, in these respects, is very imperfect. We may only learn from it the necessity of rules, wherever men have any intercourse with each other. . . . It is impossible for men so much as to murder each other without statutes, and maxims. . . .

. . . In puzzle-solving, a person [has] to think of himself in his capacity as an *agent,* and from that perspective to try to make things come out right. We [might also say] that he [has] to think of what the realization of the goal might mean to *him,* that is, he [has] to have some *value* in mind which would (or could) help him to assess the outcome of his activity.[7] We would now like to suggest that one of the "points" of games of chance, as opposed to puzzles, is that games of chance make clearer and more apparent the relation of agents to patients (adopting classical philosophical terminology). A "patient" is one to whom something is done: a recipient of an action. And we contend that in playing games of chance, we are setting afoot certain events of which the outcome to *us* is not known (though we do place a *value* on the outcome). In the same way that puzzles, as we have argued earlier, are models of problem-solving, so games of chance are models of situations in which the outcomes to the patient are not predictable.

Upshot: it is necessary for human beings, if they use both puzzles and games of chance, to be able to adopt at least two per-

[6] Hume, D., *Enquiries Concerning the Human Understanding and Concerning the Principles of Morals* (Selby-Bigge, 2nd edition), Oxford: Clarendon, 1951, p. 210.

[7] This point is hardly new. Santayana . . . says: "Reason is as old as man and as prevalent as human nature; for we should not recognise an animal to be human unless his instincts were to some degree conscious of their *ends* and rendered his ideas in that measure relevant to conduct." (Italics ours.) [*The Life of Reason: Reason in Common Sense,* 2d ed., New York: Scribner, 1932, p. 4.—Ed.]

spectives: that of *agent,* who might act, or set chains of events going, and that of *patient,* on whom actions initiated by themselves or others might impinge.

We therefore posit at least two systems of perspectives for human beings: (1) a system of *goals,* which are related to possibilities for action, and (2) a system of *values,* which are related to the possible outcomes of action for the actor. Each human being must be able to take both of these perspectives: goal-directed (or *actor*), and value-directed (or *patient*). These might coincide; we assume in some rat experiments that the goal is the food, and the value is eating it, so that rats eat the goal, with a result of value to the rat. But the existence of puzzles and games of chance may be an indication that human beings are a little more subtle, since one thinks of them as *reaching,* rather than eating, their goals.

So we are at least even with rats.

But so far as we know, rats have neither games of strategy, nor music, nor art, in any very significant sense. Since we have found both games of strategy and aesthetic objects on earth, we now pause to consider the differences between men and rats.

It is true that there are some psychological (we would prefer to say "philosophical") positions according to which there are no important differences between men and rats. Such we consider naive behaviorism to be (you give them some inputs; they give you some outputs). But we can tell men and rats apart very easily, and not *simply* because they do not look alike. There are, from the point of view we now wish to explain, more important differences. Being human requires not only goal-sensitivity, together with goal-directedness, but also some other abilities. So we move on to consider . . . games of strategy.

We note first that nothing we have said so far is incompatible with a solipsistic stance. Even the silliest solipsist sees that *he* exists as an agent, and that things happen to *him* as a patient, even though he supposes that all the rest of us are figments of his imagination. But in the case of games of strategy, this attitude will not do. One *can* adopt it for games of strategy, but von Neumann's theory [8] would indicate that one then would not be in the best position to win.

[8] Neumann, J. von. "Zur Theorie der Gesellschaftsspiele," *Mathematische Annalen,* C (1928), 295–320.

To play games of strategy seems to require that, in addition to the agent and patient perspectives, we must be able to "see ourselves as ithers see us" (Burns [9]). That is, we must recognize that ladies, unlike lice, are analyzing us much as we are analyzing them. For lack of better terminology we entitle this third perspective the *reciprocal perspective*.

Implicit in the idea that I recognize, or take account of, the fact that there are other human beings who *also* have agent and patient perspectives, is the notion that they are looking at me as I am looking at them. I must be able to evaluate my own behavior, not only from my own agent-patient point of view, but also from the agent-patient points of view (as well as I can understand them) of others. When I act, I have to see (a) what possibilities are open for myself as agent, (b) what the consequences are likely to be for me as patient, and (c) what the consequences are likely to be for the other fellow as patient, and how he is likely to react to the situation as agent—and all this in the knowledge that he probably is doing the same thing to me. In this sense each of us is "represented" as a personality in each. We cannot get along socially without taking each other into account as *social* human beings.

At the very least it seems obvious that games of strategy give us opportunities for endless practice in viewing our actions from all three of these points of view, always recognizing the existence of other beings like ourselves. What the reciprocal perspective allows us to do is to reciprocate. In a play of the game of chess, for example, we reciprocate in just the sense that we take each other's actions into account, and guide our own behavior by considering not only what our Knight can do, but what his Queen can do, and what the outcome of the game will be.

It is hard to see how human beings could handle games of strategy, as we find them on earth, without being able to take account of the agent-patient perspectives of *others*. Some such ability would seem necessary for games of strategy. We might sometimes confuse the various "parts" of the personalities involved, or we may sometimes ignore a part of someone else—usually to our peril: if we do not sufficiently take into account another's role as agent or patient, we might lose a knight which is pinned to the King. But unless we could keep these various perspectives "in

[9] Burns, R. "To a louse," in *Poems chiefly in the Scottish dialect*. Kilmarnock, 1786.

perspective," it would seem difficult to understand how we could play at all. . . .

But . . . do not animals also interact in the sense that they guide their own behavior in part by the behavior of their colleagues? Consider the following example of George Herbert Mead's: [10]

> The act of each dog becomes the stimulus to the other dog for his response. There is then a relationship between these two; and as the act is responded to by the other dog, it, in turn, undergoes change. The very fact that the dog is ready to attack another becomes a stimulus to the other dog to change his own position or his own attitude. He has not sooner done this than the change of attitude in the second dog in turn causes the first dog to change his attitude. We have here a conversation of gestures. They are not, however, gestures in the sense that they are significant. We do not assume that the dog says to himself, "If the animal comes from this direction he is going to spring at my throat and I will turn in such a way." What does take place is an actual change in his own position due to the direction of the approach of the other dog.

Now it may be debatable whether or not a dog, in approaching a bone, actually *takes the role of* another dog doing the same. (We, along with Mead, think it does not, in any significant sense, but the matter hardly seems worth arguing, in view of the vagueness of the issues.) But one thing seems perfectly clear: one cannot imagine a dog saying, or even thinking, "Tut, tut, tut; that is not in accordance with the rules." We can of course imagine a dog being *surprised* by some unexpected event which "breaks rules" with which the dog is familiar; but the surprise is rather more like the surprise we feel at a sudden and unexpected earthquake, than the surprise we feel when a close friend suddenly slips a knife between our ribs. The former is ' a physical sort of surprise, and we are all partially prepared for those. But the latter are social surprises, and are available to dogs only in the same metaphorical sense that household pets are "people."

We have referred to the earthquake surprise as "physical," and the being-knifed-by-a-friend surprise as "social," and though we are not very clear as to what this distinction involves, we will still try to give an account of it.

[10] Mead, *op. cit.*, pp. 42–43.—Ed.

It does not make much sense to say that the earth "is not supposed to" (in the sense of "ought not") quake. We can all see that it would be nicer if the earth did not quake, or if volcanoes did not erupt; things like this hurt people. But if one were to say "volcanoes ought not erupt," in any sense which involved adherence to rules on the part of volcanoes, it would be hard to attach any sense to the utterance. It would be odd if, after the burial of Pompeii, someone were to shake a finger at Mt. Vesuvius and say in a severe voice, "Sceleste, sceleste, Vesuvi!"

It *would* be appropriate, however, to treat our treacherous ex-friend in this way. *All of us* can see what "Et tu, Brute," means, once the story and the Latin are explained. What it means is simply that friends are not supposed to do that kind of thing to one another. Which is to say that the notion of "friendship" involves conducting oneself according to certain *rules*. (We do not specify these for reasons which ought to be obvious: the problem is too difficult.)

Whatever feelings the treachery of our *own* friend in these circumstances might engender, it seems perfectly clear that all of us can see how Caesar might have felt—not about the wound, that is, but the treachery. And note that this understanding really has nothing to do with Caesar, Brutus, or ourselves (ourselves viewed as agents, patients, or from the reciprocal perspective of anyone we know). We could substitute "Caesar" for "Brutus," and "Brutus" for "Caesar" throughout the whole play, without losing anything except such historical accuracy as the play has. We seem to be able to look at the matter, thinking not so much about Caesar or Brutus, or ourselves as individuals, but rather of the *role* of a friend, and the obligations it lays on anyone whatever, including ourselves. We are by such considerations led to postulate the existence of a fourth (and, we are happy to say, final) social human perspective, namely, that of an umpire—a detached standpoint from which we decide whether rules have or have not been broken.

It is important to see that the umpire's perspective can be applied to our own behavior as well as to that of others. When so applied, it goes under the name "conscience." When our conscience bothers us, it is, we claim, because we are able to look at our own actions, not only from the point of view of ourselves as agents, or patients, or from the reciprocal point of view of other individuals, but also from the point of view of a third party, who was really not there—namely, from the perspective of the umpire,[11] who is watching to see that the play goes fairly. . . .

. . . We are inclined to guess that all the elements required for games of strategy are present when we contemplate or enjoy aesthetic objects, but again that the emphasis is different. When we watch a performance of Sheridan's *The Rivals*, two principal things seem to be involved: (1) our perspectives as patient to the spectacle, from which we feel enjoyment, or illumination, or any of the emotions appropriate to appreciation (or lack of it) of a play; and (2) our perspectives as referees, or umpires; i.e., as critics, who understand in an impersonal way the rules for enacting *The Rivals*, the rules for competent acting, and who can tell whether or not the affair is coming off properly—with the appropriate emotions of consternation, fright, or delight.

It seems clear, at any rate, that our perspectives as agents are involved in aesthetic responses in a very minimal way, unless we happen to be the performers, or we are on a showboat, where hissing the villain is good form. And it seems equally clear that the reciprocal perspective—looking at ourselves from the point of view of another person—is involved at best vicariously. But the way in which the performance is carried on (that is, the extent to which performers follow the rules, where rules are looked at from a referee's point of view), seems to be of much more importance in encounters with aesthetic objects.

[11] The term "umpire" is of some interest. It derives from old French, *nomper*, from *non* not, and *per* peer or equal. I.e., the umpire's role is that of a third party and not that of a fellow interactor. (*Umpire*, without initial *n-*, arose through the incorrect division of *a numpire* as *an umpire*.)

JAMES AGEE

# The Interviewer Received at Night

*Moore and Anderson indicate that there are affinities between the social sciences and the humanities worth keeping up. In both fields alert thinking confronts the same complications—typical and untypical—of human personality and social interaction. The following selection is an example of literary art, drawn from a factual record of field observations conducted among white tenant farmers in Alabama during the thirties. The episode described took place after Agee, who had briefly visited the Gudgers earlier in the day, unexpectedly came back at night to seek shelter.*

*James Agee (1909–1955) was one of the most admired American writers of his time. Besides collaborating (with Walker Evans, the photographer) on the unique and moving book from which this episode is taken, he distinguished himself as a poet and novelist (especially in A Death in the Family, published posthumously [New York: McDowell, Obolensky, 1957]).*

All this while we are talking some: short of exact recording, which is beyond my memory, I can hardly say how: the forms of these plainest and most casual actions are the hardest I can conceive of to set down straight as they happen; and each is somewhat more beautiful and more valuable, I feel, than, say, the sonnet form. This form was one in which two plain people and one complex one who scarcely know each other discourse while one eats and the others wait for him to finish so they may get back to bed: it has the rhythms and inflections of this triple shyness, of sleepiness, of fast eating, of minds in the influence of lamplight between pine walls, of talk which means little or nothing of itself and much in its inflections: What is the use? What is there I can do about it? Let me try just a few of the surfaces instead. Just in the fact that they were drawn up out of bed to do me this natural kindness, one in overalls and one in a house dress slid on over nakedness, and were sitting here, a man and his wife, in an hour whose lateness is uncommon to them, there is a particular sort of intimacy between the three of us which is not of our creating and which has nothing to do with our talk, yet which is increased in our tones of voice, in small quiet turns of humor, in glances of the eyes, in ways even that I eat my food, in their knowledge how truly friendly I feel toward them, and how seriously I am concerned to have caused them bother, and to let them be done with this bother as quickly as possible. And the best in this—it will be hard to explain unless you know something of women in this civilization—is the experiencing of warmth and of intimacy toward a man and his wife at the same time (for this would seldom happen, it being the business of a wife to serve and to withdraw). I felt such an honor in her not just staying at more distance, waiting to clear up after me, but sitting near, almost equal in balance with her husband, and actually talking; and I began even through her deep exhaustion to see such pleasant and seldom warmth growing in her, in this shifted status and acceptance in it, and such a kindly and surprised current of warmth increasing through this between her husband and her, a new light and gentle novelty spreading a prettiness in her face that, beyond a first expostulation that she get back to her rest and leave me to clean off the table, I not only scarcely worried for her tiredness, or her husband's, but even somewhat prolonged the while we sat there, shamed though I was to do so, and they wakened, and warmed to talking, even while fatigue so much more heavily weighed them under, till it became in the scale of their sleeping an almost scandalously late-night conversation, in which we were all leaned toward each other in the lamplight secretly examining the growth of friendliness in one another's faces, they opening further speaking as often as I and more often: while nevertheless there stole up my quiet delight from the pit of my stomach a cold and sickening shame to be keeping them up, a feeling I had mistaken their interest and their friendliness, that it was only a desperate and nearly broken patience in a trap I had imposed in abuse of their goodness; and I broke through a little wait in what we were speaking, to say how sorry and ashamed I was, and that we must get to sleep; and this they received so genuinely, so kindly, that even in their exhaustion I was immediately healed, and held no fear of their feelings about it: and we drew back our chairs and got up and she cleared the table (no, beyond quickly stacking my dishes toward her I could not offer even to help her with this) and there followed a simple set of transitions which are beautiful in my remembrance and which I can scarcely set down: a telling me where I would sleep, in the front room; a spreading of pallets on the floor of the back bedroom; a waking and bringing-in of the children from their sleeping on the bed I was to have: they came sleepwalking, along bare floor toward lamplight, framed in the lighted upright planks of the door: the yielding-over to me of the lamp, which I accepted (there are courtesies you accept, though you are ashamed to), provided they should have used it first to get themselves to bed: they give me, meanwhile, their little tin night-light, which looks like the minutest kind of Roman lamp: I say good night to Mrs. Gudger and she to me, smiling sleepily and sadly in a way I cannot deduce, and goes on in; I button my door, that leads into their bedroom, and wait in this front room, new to me, with my night-light, sitting on the edge of the child-warmed bed, looking at the little sketches of carpentry I can see in my faint light, and at the light under their door and through seams in the wall, while in a confusion of shufflings and of muted voices which overspreads the sleeping of children like quiet wings; and rustlings of cloth, and sounding of bedsprings, they restore themselves for sleeping: then a shuffling, a sliding of light, a soft knock at the door; I come to it; Gudger and I exchange our lamps, speaking few words in nearly inaudible voices, while beyond his shoulder I feel the deep dark breathing a soft and quiet prostration of bodies: All right in year hain't you?—Ah, sure, fine. Sure am.—Annie Mae told me to say, she's sorry she ain't got no clean sheet, but just have to (*oh, no!*) make out best way you can.—Oh, no. No. You tell her I certainly do thank her, but, no, I'll be fine like this, *fine* like this—She just don't got none tell she does a warshin.—Sure; sure; I wouldn't want to dirty up a clean sheet for you, one night. Thanks a lot. Door, right head a yer bed, if you want to git out. I look, and nod:

Yeah; thanks.

Night:

Night:

The door draws shut.

HERBERT A. SIMON

# Mathematical Constructions
# in Social Science

*Creative thinking in the social sciences may, of course, take mathematical
or experimental lines as well as literary ones. In the following selection,
Simon offers a variety of mathematical representations of human activity,
arranging his illustrations in a significant order that leads from "optimizing" models familiar in economics to "adaptive" models initially designed
for topics in psychology and sociology.*

*(Students without mathematics need not be daunted by the formulas that
Simon uses. Most of what he is saying can be gathered without reading
the more complicated formulas; and these are simple enough to be read
by anyone who will spend half an hour with a calculus textbook or with
a popular account of the calculus, such as the one in Chapter 15 of Morris
Kline's* Mathematics in Western Culture *[New York: Oxford University
Press, 1953].)*

*Herbert A. Simon (1916– ), professor of administration and psy-
chology at Carnegie Institute of Technology, might be classified by his
interests and researches equally well as a political scientist, psychologist,
sociologist, economist—and philosopher.*

## SECTION I. MODELS OF OPTIMIZATION

It is my aim in this paper to discuss some problems of strategy
in theory construction in the social sciences. To put the matter more
modestly, I should like to set forth, illustrate, and discuss some of
the basic strategic considerations that have guided my own work
in the formulation of theories—and particularly mathematical theories—of various aspects of human behavior.

The undertaking requires some preface. First, I should like to
rule out of bounds the question of whether mathematics has any
business in the social sciences. I will simply assert, with J. Willard

Gibbs,[1] that mathematics is a language; it is a language that sometimes makes things clearer to me than do other languages, and that sometimes helps me discover things that I have been unable to discover with the use of other languages. What the contribution of mathematics will be to the social sciences can perhaps be more fruitfully evaluated some generations hence when that contribution —if any—has been made.

Second, we shall be concerned with *applied* mathematics, and hence we shall be as concerned with the field of application as with mathematics itself. The strategy of mathematical theorizing must come primarily from the field about which the theorizing is to be done. The aim of a language is to say something—and not merely to say something about the language itself. Mathematical social science is, first and foremost, social science. If it is bad social science (i.e., empirically false), the fact that it is good mathematics (i.e., logically consistent) should provide little comfort. . . .

## Models of Rational Behavior

As far as economic and administrative theory are concerned, man has been conceived primarily as a rational animal. The concept of rationality has played a prominent, but much less central, role in the other social sciences. Since economics, of all the social sciences, has had by far the greatest assistance from mathematics, it is not surprising that models of rational behavior are far more advanced than mathematical models of other aspects of behavior.

The most advanced theories, both verbal and mathematical, of rational behavior are those that employ as their central concepts the notions of: (1) a set of alternative courses of action presented to the individual's choice; (2) knowledge and information that permit the individual to predict the consequences of choosing any alternative; and (3) a criterion for determining which set of consequences he prefers.[2] In these theories rationality consists in selecting that course of action which leads to the set of consequences most preferred. (At a later point of our discussion we will see that this

---

[1] American mathematical physicist (1839–1903).—Ed.

[2] For an extended (verbal) discussion of this model, and a comparison with the less satisfactory "means-ends" model employed by Parsons, Tolman and others, see H. A. Simon, *Administrative Behavior* (New York: Macmillan, 1947), ch. 4. *Cf.* Paul A. Samuelson, *Foundations of Economic Analysis* (Cambridge: Harvard U. Press, 1947), pp. 21–3, 97–8.

definition of rationality is somewhat too restrictive, but we may accept it temporarily as a starting point for analysis.)

Practically the whole of classical economic theory is constructed within the framework of this model. As an example of a mathematical version of it, which will serve to indicate how a verbal theory can be mathematized, we may take a very simple model of the theory of the firm. In this simple example there is a single rational human being, an "entrepreneur" who is operating a firm that manufactures a single product from a single raw material. (1) The alternatives open to the entrepreneur are to employ more or less of the raw material. (2) The consequences of a given course of action are that he will incur a cost (determined by the price of the raw material, and the quantity used), and he will receive a revenue (determined by the price of the product, and the quantity produced with the given amount of raw material). We assume that he knows the price at which any specified amount of raw material can be bought, the price at which any specified amount of product can be sold, and the maximum amount of product that can be produced from a given amount of raw material. That is, he knows his "supply curve," his "demand curve," and his "production function." (In this model, the supplier and the consumer need not be regarded as rational human beings, their behavior being specified and known.) (3) The entrepreneur's criterion is that he wishes the largest possible profit—the largest attainable difference between total revenue and cost of production.

*The Mathematical Translation.* In the language of mathematics, let y be the quantity of product made, and x the quantity of raw material bought. Let $p = p(y)$ be the price of the product, which is assumed to depend on the quantity sold; and $P = P(x)$ be the price of the raw material, assumed to depend on the quantity bought. Let the quantity of product obtainable from a given quantity of raw material be given by $y = f(x)$. Then the entrepreneur's alternatives are a range of values of x. The revenue, $yp(y) = f(x)p(f(x))$, and the cost $xP(x)$, are the consequences which can be calculated when x is known. The criterion is to maximize the profit, $\pi = yp(y) - xP(x)$, regarded as a function of x. The rational behavior is given by the well-known "marginal" condition, stated for small changes in $\pi$ contingent upon small changes in x,

$$\frac{d\pi}{dx} = \frac{df(x)}{dx} p[f(x)] + f(x) \frac{dp}{dy} \frac{df(x)}{dx} - P(x) - x \frac{dP}{dx} = 0 \qquad (1),$$

where the middle expression is arrived at by a straightforward application of the differential calculus to the expression $yp(y) - xP(x)$.

Translating this equation back into English (without trying to translate it term by term), it says that the rational entrepreneur will fix his output at the point where marginal cost equals marginal revenue.

Several features of this model deserve notice, as generally characteristic of models of rational behavior. Certain variables—in this case x—are regarded as "strategic" variables, controllable by a rational being. Other variables—in this case $\pi$—are the criterion, and measure of the goal he is seeking. The limits of attainment are set by conditions outside his control—relationships he must accept—which determine the value of the criterion as a function of the strategic variable. The problem of rationality then becomes a problem in maximization—to find the greatest value of the criterion, regarded as a function of the strategic variables.

*Significance of the Limits of Rationality.* If we regard this model as a description of the actual behavior of some entrepreneur, we see that if we are to predict his behavior, the knowledge that he is rational is only a small part—almost an insignificant part—of the information that we require. His intention to be rational leads to particular behavior only in the context of conditions in which his behavior takes place. These conditions include both (1) the limits expressed by the demand curve, the supply curve, and the production function—we might regard these as the limits of his "abilities" in the situation—and (2) the limits expressed by the criterion function. The criterion (regarded as a "final end") is itself not an object of rational calculation, but a given. The model would be equally a model of rational behavior if the entrepreneur chose to maximize his losses, or his gross revenue instead of his profit.

Indeed, our principal use for such models is in predicting how the entrepreneur's behavior will be affected by a change in the environment that conditions or "bounds" his rationality. For example, we may wish to predict how the price and output of the product will be altered, assuming the entrepreneur always to behave rationally, if there occurs a shift in the demand function. To do this, we can regard the price of the product, p, as depending both on the quantity sold, y, and upon a parameter (i.e., a coefficient regarded as constant in the short run, but as possibly varying in the long run), a, which may vary, for example, with changes in consumers' tastes:

$p = p(y,a)$. Each change in a shifts the whole demand curve—relating p to y—to right or left. If we follow the maximizing procedure previously described for finding the optimal value of x, this value will now depend on a—that is, a will in general appear in equation (1). Hence, we can regard equation (1) as a statement of relationship between x and a—a statement of how production, under the assumption of the entrepreneur's rationality, will vary with shifts in demand.

We may summarize our discussion to this point by saying: that a simple model of rational behavior leads quite naturally to maximizing procedures and, in mathematical translation, to the methods of the differential calculus; and that the specific features of interest in any particular model arise primarily from the particular conditions under which rationality is exercised. This second point perhaps deserves to be dignified as a . . . canon of strategy: *In mathematical models incorporating rational and non-rational aspects of behavior, the non-rational aspects can be imbedded in the model as the limiting conditions that "bound" the area of rational adjustment. . . .*

*Reaction Time—Rationality and Dynamics.* . . . In our simple model of the theory of the firm, the entrepreneur is assumed to know not only the shape of the demand curve, but also its position at any given time—i.e., the value of the parameter a. For many situations a more realistic assumption would be that he does not have this detailed knowledge, but only discovers his optimal position by experimenting and learning on the basis of his experience and his mistakes. For example, he might have some information about marginal costs and marginal revenue, but only in the neighborhood of the position in which he is actually operating. He might then adopt the rule of behavior that he will continue to increase his output so long as his marginal revenue is in excess of marginal cost, and decrease it whenever he finds marginal cost in excess of marginal revenue. In equations, the assumption is:

$$\frac{dx}{dt} = b \left\{ \frac{df(x)}{dx} \, p \, [f(x)] + f(x) \, \frac{dp}{dy} \, \frac{df(x)}{dx} - P(x) - x \, \frac{dP}{dx} \right\},$$

$$(b > 0). \qquad (2)$$

Given equation (1), $b = \frac{dx}{dt} \Big/ \frac{d\pi}{dx}$. The size of this ratio will vary for reasons that we shall not go into. So long, however, as it is

greater than 0, the entrepreneur will find it profitable to add incre-
ments to the quantity of x that he is using; if after any such addition,
it still remains greater than 0, he will be well advised to add another
increment of x.

Now if "other conditions" like the parameter a remain reasonably steady, and if the system satisfies certain other stability
requirements, it turns out that the optimal solution, in the sense
of equation (1), is actually the stable equilibrium position of
the time path described by equation (2). When this is true, equation (2) may be taken as a definition of rational behavior under the
restrictions of information that have been assumed. *How* rational
it is, will depend, of course, on the size of the coefficient b, which
measures the adjustment rate, for if this coefficient is large the
adjustment and the approach to the equilibrium will be rapid,
while if b is small, the approach will be slow. If, now, a fluctu-
ates moderately (there are shifts from time to time in demand),
a large b will prevent the entrepreneur from ever departing very
widely from the optimal output, while a small b may permit very
wide departures, and consequent loss of profit.

The difference between the kind of rationality depicted in equation (1) and the kind depicted in equation (2) might be described
as follows. Two popcorn men are vending their wares on a very
large county fair ground. Their profits will depend on keeping their
wagons in the part of the fair ground where as dense a crowd as
possible has assembled. The crowd is in continual motion. The
first popcorn man has radio equipment on his wagon on which he
has arranged to receive from all parts of the fair ground frequent
reports on the size of the crowd. As soon as he learns where it is
densest, he speeds to that part of the ground. The second popcorn
man has less modern equipment. He keeps his cart in motion in the
direction of increasing density of the crowd, and away from the
direction of decreasing density. . . .

*Optimizing versus Adaptive Behavior.* As we move from the static
model to the dynamic, our original definition of rationality (selection of that course of action which leads to the set of consequences
most preferred) becomes somewhat too restrictive. On the one
hand, we may build the concept of rationality, as in the earlier
models, upon the ability of the individual to discover a "best" situation and to move toward it, either instantaneously (as in the static
models) or gradually (as in the dynamic). On the other hand,

## Motivation and Learning

In psychological formulations of adaptive human behavior, the concepts of motivation and learning are central.[4] The notion of motivation is closely connected with the "criterion" in the models of optimization, while learning is connected with changes in such limitations on rationality as "state of information" and "technology." In the present model we shall not attempt any further exact translation from the previous concepts, but will start afresh.

*The "Berlitz" Model.* We suppose that there is an activity in which an individual engages from time to time, and that he can engage in varying amounts of it each day. As he engages in it, it becomes progressively easier for him (this is our "learning" assumption). To the extent that he finds it pleasant, he engages in it more frequently; to the extent he finds it unpleasant, he engages in it less frequently. Its pleasantness depends on how easy it is for him. (The latter two statements comprise our "motivation" assumption.)

As a concrete example, we may suppose that our individual has subscribed to a correspondence course to learn French by the Berlitz method. Each day he spends a certain amount of time in practice. As he practices, the language becomes easier; so long as the difficulty is greater than a certain level, he finds the work unpleasant, and tends to shorten his practice session. (We assume our student to be a kind of hedonist.) If he reaches a certain level of skill, however, the work becomes pleasant, and he will tend to practice for a longer period.

Let $x(t)$ be the rate (say, in hours per day) at which the activity is being performed at time t. Let $D(t)$ be the level of difficulty, and let us assume (learning) that *if* the practice rate were held constant, the difficulty would decrease logarithmically with time, the speed of the logarithmic decrease being proportional to the practice rate. We do not need to make assumptions quite as special as this, but they will simplify our discussion and it will be easy enough to see how they can be generalized. Since the actual practice rate may vary with time, we state the assumption thus:

$$d(\log D)/dt = (1/D)dD/dt = -ax(t), \tag{7}$$

[4] The contrast between the optimizing man of the economists and the adaptive man of the psychologists is discussed in Simon, *Administrative Behavior*, chapter 4 . . . and chapter 5.

where a $> 0$ is a constant. Let us assume that at any given level of difficulty, practice is pleasurable up to a certain point, and unpleasant beyond that point, and that $x = \bar{x}(D)$ is this satiation level of activity, for any particular level, D, of difficulty. We assume then (motivation) that the practice rate will increase when practice is pleasurable, decrease when it is unpleasant, thus:

$$dx/dt = -b(x - \bar{x}),\qquad\qquad\qquad (8)$$

where b is another positive constant. The two equations for dD/dt and dx/dt permit us to predict the time paths of D and x if we know their initial values, $D_0$ and $x_0$ at time $t_0$. Several representative time paths are shown in Figure 1.

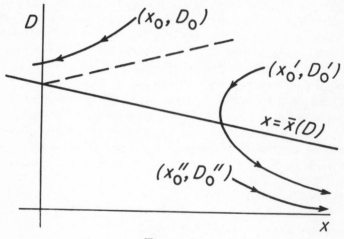

Figure 1

The figure shows that whether our student eventually becomes discouraged and fails to complete his course, or whether he is successful in learning French depends on his starting point (and, of course, on the relative magnitudes of a and b and the shape of $\bar{x}(D)$). The value of $D_0$ represents the difficulty of the language to him at the outset, and $x_0$ the amount of time he initially devotes to practice. If the point $(x_0, D_0)$ lies above the dotted line, he will ultimately become discouraged and give up his lessons; if, instead, he begins at $(x'_0, D'_0)$, between the dotted line and the line $x = \bar{x}(D)$, he will suffer some discouragement at the outset, but practice will ultimately become pleasant and he will learn the language. If he begins at $(x''_0, D''_0)$, practice will be pleasant from the outset, and he will learn.

Clearly one would want to refine this model before trying to verify it from actual situations, but even in its highly simple form it exhibits some of the qualitative features we would expect to find in such situations, and illustrates in what a natural manner differential equations can be employed in a model of adaptive behavior.

*Prediction and Verification.* One interesting feature of a model of this sort is that it permits qualitative predictions to be made that are very easy to test empirically. We do not need to trace out in detail the time path of the system, but merely to observe whether the activity terminates before learning was completed, or whether it ends in mastery of the language. With such observations we can test, over a sample of cases, a prediction like: the activity is likely to persist until learning has been achieved only if the initial rate of practice is above a certain critical level.

*Multiple Equilibria.* Another feature of importance is that the model allows us to deal with behavioral or social systems in which both intermittent forces, which act for a brief period, and continuously acting forces are at play. The intermittent force in this case would be the individual's decision to subscribe to the language course and devote a certain amount of time to practice (i.e., the determinants of the initial position). The continuous forces would be the process of learning and the varying motivation as the resolution was actually carried out (i.e., the forces determining the path from the initial position). A Spencer would say that the final outcome is determined by the continuous interplay of forces immanent in the behavioral interaction itself; a Bentham would say that the outcome is determined by the intermittent intervention—the determination of the initial conditions.[5] The two views are in fact not contradictory provided the system has more than one position of final equilibrium. In this case an intervention can "jar" the system from one position of equilibrium to another.

[5] See William Archibald Dunning, *A History of Political Theories: From Rousseau to Spencer* (New York: Macmillan, 1920), pp. 395–402 [on Spencer and his conception of evolutionary changes in "the relative scope and intensity" of "two species of cooperation"—"conscious and involuntary" and "spontaneous and voluntary"], pp. 211–24 [on Bentham, emphasizing his treatment of "calculated self-interest" as the "all-pervading motive of human action"].

A possible application of this notion is to the theory of political and social "reform" movements. It is notorious that such movements are short-lived, at least in their active and influential phases. If they are effective, it must be through disturbance of a system of forces previously in equilibrium, and a sufficient shift in initial conditions to permit the system to move toward a new equilibrium with a different stable constellation of forces.

There would seem to be a wide class of social phenomena that could be studied in terms of a model embodying this feature of multiple equilbria. Gunnar Myrdal's theory of social change appears to be of this sort, as do most theories of revolution.[6] The relationship between "formal" organization (which operates in considerable part through intermittent pressures) and "informal" organization might also be expressed in these terms.

*A Social Interpretation of the "Berlitz" Model.* It might appear that we are not justified in discussing the applicability to social systems of a model that represents, after all, the behavior of a single human being. In fact, however, the writer was originally led to construct this model in order to represent a social situation. In an organization where accountants were given the task of providing accounting information to operating executives, it was found that if understanding between accountants and operators was good, they tended to communicate frequently with each other; when it was bad, less frequently. Moreover, frequent communication, by helping them understand each others' languages, made communication easier. By renaming the variable x "frequency of communication between accountants and operators," and the variable D "difficulty of communication between accountants and operators," we obtain in the model a clear representation of this social system. . . .

### Equilibrium in Group Interaction

The previous section suggests that in the study of human and social adaptive systems we may be interested not only in the mechanism of adaptation, but also in the possible states of equilibrium of the system. In the present section we will examine a system of social interaction with primary emphasis on equilibrium . . .

*The Homans Model.* The system to be examined· has some intrin-

[6] See Gunnar Myrdal, *An American Dilemma* (New York: Harper, 1944), Appendix 3. While Myrdal does not speak explicitly of multiple equilibria this seems to be an implicit element of his model.

sic interest in that it appears to represent fairly well in a formal model some of the theoretical relations postulated by George Homans in *The Human Group*.[7] Homans' system contains four variables (his treatment of them is, of course, verbal rather than mathematical):

(1) The intensity of interaction (or communication) among the members of a group; we will designate it by $T(t)$.

(2) The amount of friendliness (or group identification) among group members; we will designate it by $I(t)$.

(3) The total amount of activity carried on by a member of the group; we will designate it by $W(t)$.

(4) The amount of activity imposed on the group by its external environment (the amount required for its survival); we will designate it by $F(t)$. (Homans also calls it the activity required for survival, the "external system.")

Each of the variables is written as a function of time, and each of the first three is supposed to be some kind of average of the levels for the individual members of the group. Homans nowhere explicitly states his postulates regarding the interrelations of these variables, but the postulates he actually employs would seem to be contained in the following statements:

"If the scheme of activities is changed, the scheme of interaction will, in general, change also, and vice versa."

"Persons who interact frequently with one another tend to like one another."

"If the interactions between the members of a group are frequent in the external system, sentiments of liking will grow up between them, and these sentiments will lead in turn to further interaction over and above the interactions of external system."

"Persons who feel sentiments of liking for one another will express those sentiments in activities over and above the activities of the external system, and these activities may further strengthen the sentiments of liking."

"The more frequently persons interact with one another, the more alike in some respects both their activities and their sentiments tend to become."

[7] (New York: Harcourt, Brace, 1950). A more detailed discussion of the formal model of Homans' system is presented in Simon, "A Formal Theory of Interaction in Social Groups," *American Sociological Review*, April 1952, pp. 202–211.

*A Mathematical Translation.* Now these five statements can be approximately translated into three equations among our four variables. The first equation will be algebraic—representing an "instantaneous" or very rapid adjustment. The other two will be differential equations determining paths over time.

$$T = a_1 I + a_2 W \tag{9}$$

$$\frac{dI}{dt} = b (T - \beta I) \tag{10}$$

$$\frac{dW}{dt} = c_1 (I - \gamma W) + c_2 (F - W) \tag{11}$$

The first equation may be translated, roughly: interaction will be produced by friendliness and/or group activity. The second: friendliness will tend to increase or decrease as the amount of interaction is disproportionately large or disproportionately small, respectively, in relation to the existing level of friendliness. (The two variables will be in adjstment when $T = \beta I$.) The third: group activity will tend to increase as the level of friendliness is high relative to the existing level of activity (the two being in equilibrium when $I = \gamma W$), and as the requirements of the external system are high relative to the existing level of activity, otherwise group activity will tend to decrease.

By studying these translations—or better, by studying the equations themselves—in relation to Homans' postulates, the reader can judge for himself how well we have succeeded in capturing the essential features of Homans' system in our equations. In any event it is unnecessary to concern ourselves here with the exactness of the representation or the empirical correctness of his postulates.

Now systems of the kind we have just written down (linear differential equations with constant coefficients) are well known to the mathematician, and he can provide us with a well-stocked kit of tools for analysing their behavior. Without going into details of method or result, it may be stated that he can easily find: (1) the equilibrium position of this system, (2) the conditions under which this equilibrium is stable and unstable, and (3) the precise time path the system will follow from any initial position.

*Social Disintegration.* Among the conclusions that can be drawn from the purely mathematical properties of the system is the following:

If the system represented by equations (9)–(11) is dynamically stable, then as the system of externally imposed activities, F, decreases toward zero, the amounts of interaction, friendliness, and group activity will decrease toward zero (with a lag).

But this is precisely the hypothesis that Homans employs to explain social disintegration in Hilltown, and to explain the difference in extension between the primitive and modern family. Our formal model permits us to demonstrate rigorously that this is not an independent hypothesis, but follows logically from the other postulates if only the system is assumed to be dynamically stable.

*Morale and "Anomie".* We will cite one further example of the conclusions that mathematical reasoning permits us to draw from the model. One of Homans' empirical statements is that a social group will tend to develop a system of activities more elaborate than that needed to satisfy the requirements of the external system. In one sense we have already incorporated this statement in equation (11)—for this equation says that W will tend to increase not only if F is greater than W, but also when I is greater than $\gamma W$. That is, friendliness, as well as external requirements can be a source of group activity. But does it follow from this that, when the system has attained equilibrium, W will be greater than F?

Let us define a group as possessing "positive morale" if, when the group is in a state of equilibrium, W exceeds F—the actual level of activity is higher than that required for survival. When this condition is not satisfied, we will say that the group possesses "negative morale." It can be shown from equations (9)–(11) that the group will possess positive morale if and only if $a_2 > \gamma(\beta - a_1)$. To see what the condition means we note that, in particular, it will be satisfied if $a_2$ is sufficiently large—that is, if the amount of interaction required per unit of group activity is large. This can be stated in still another way: group morale will be positive if there is a sufficiently high degree of interrelation among the members' tasks, requiring much communication for their performance. But this is, in substance, the central proposition of Durkheim's theory of *anomie* [8] —a proposition that has received considerable empirical verification in work situations from the Hawthorne studies and their successors.[9] . . .

[8] See the note on Durkheim and *anomie* in the Bibliography below, p. 120, §5.—Ed.

[9] The Hawthorne studies, carried out at the Hawthorne plant in Chicago of the Western Electric Co., dealt with the effects on work group morale and productivity of experimentally varied working conditions. See Elton Mayo, *The Human Problems of an Industrial Civilization* (New York: The Macmillan Co., 1933); also Homans, *op. cit.*, chap. 3.—Ed.

[FINAL COMMENT]

Our general procedure in this paper has been to start with theories of optimizing behavior—theories that incorporate the fewest possible limits on rationality. We have then progressively diluted the requirements of rationality—or stated otherwise, have imposed successive limitations. In this way we have progressed from simple processes of maximization to much more complex processes of adaptive (and even of "motivated" and "learned") behavior.

With each additional limitation we have been confronted with choices—we have had to make more and more assumptions as to the characteristics of actual human behavior. Hence it is not surprising that at each step we have (at least potentially) gained realism, but lost certainty. Empirical research has not progressed to the point where we can make assured choices among alternative assumptions; and mathematical analysis of the models has not progressed to the point where we can handle simultaneously all of the complications we should like to incorporate.

What can we conclude about the present state and future prospects of this kind of model-building? We do not pretend to have surveyed all, or even most, of the existent attempts at mathematization. . . . We can, however, draw several conclusions. Formalization of the systems in which highly rational and individualistic behavior is postulated has already reached a point of development where mathematical theory is displacing literary theory on the frontiers of research. Most of the things that can be said in economics can be said more easily and clearly with the language of mathematics than without it. Moreover, mathematics has already made important contributions not only to substantive theory but also to the clarification of central concepts. In particular, we have seen that the attempt to set down in mathematical form the precise assumptions of "rationality" has led to important advances in the understanding of that concept and its various possible meanings.

In areas of a more distinctly sociological or psychological character, much less has been accomplished. Even here we have seen that rather simple mathematical tools permit us to study with a high degree of clarity and rigor the assumptions underlying particular theories, the conclusions that follow from these assumptions, and the interrelations of competing theories. The tentative explorations made thus far give sufficiently good prospect of rich reward to justify further work on a much larger and more systematic scale.

# Social Science and Social Policy

*Rational policy-making calls on social science for help; and social science has largely been created in response to the needs of policy-making. But how is social science best used to serve those needs? If, as Simon implies, adaptive models are often more suitable for describing choice-behavior under ordinary conditions of limited information, one might conjecture that an adaptive model may often be more suitable for prescribing how social science is to be used. Popper argues that a piecemeal approach to policy-making deliberately limited to small departures makes it possible to use the findings of social science with reasonable confidence and simultaneously—an intimately connected matter—makes it possible for social science to draw new lessons from the effects of policies.*

## THE TECHNOLOGICAL APPROACH TO SOCIOLOGY

The term 'social technology' (and even more the term 'social engineering' [1] which will be introduced in the next section) is likely to arouse suspicion, and to repel those whom it reminds of the 'social blueprints' of the collectivist planners, or perhaps even of the 'technocrats'. I realize this danger, and so I have added the word 'piecemeal', both to off-set undesirable associations and to express my conviction that 'piecemeal tinkering' (as it is sometimes called), combined with critical analysis, is the main way to practical results in the social as well as in the natural sciences. The social sciences have developed very largely through the criticism of proposals for social improvements or, more precisely, through attempts to find out whether or not some particular economic or political action is likely to produce an expected, or desired, result.[2] This approach, which might indeed be called the classical one, is what I have in mind

From Karl R. Popper, *The Poverty of Historicism* (London: Routledge & Kegan Paul, Ltd., 1957, 2d ed., 1960; and New York: Harper Torchbooks, Harper & Row, 1964. © Karl Raimund Popper 1957, 1960. Used by permission of Routledge and the author. [Taken from pp. 58–70 of the 2d (1960) edition.]

[1] For a defence of this term, see note 6 on page 103, below.

[2] Cp. F. A. von Hayek, *Economica*, vol. XIII (1933), p. 123. '. . . economics developed mainly as the outcome of the investigation and refutation of successive Utopian proposals . . .'

when I refer to the technological approach to social science, or to 'piecemeal social technology'.

Technological problems in the field of social science may be of a 'private' or of a 'public' character. For example, investigations into the technique of business administration, or into the effects of improved working conditions upon output, belong to the first group. Investigations into the effects of prison reform or universal health insurance, or of the stabilization of prices by means of tribunals, or of the introduction of new import duties, etc., upon, say, the equalization of incomes, belong to the second group; and so do some of the most urgent practical questions of the day, such as the possibility of controlling trade cycles; or the question whether centralized 'planning', in the sense of state management of production, is compatible with an effective democratic control of the administration; or the question of how to export democracy to the Middle East.

This emphasis upon the practical technological approach does not mean that any of the theoretical problems that may arise from the analysis of the practical problems should be excluded. On the contrary, it is one of my main points that the technological approach is likely to prove fruitful in giving rise to significant problems of a purely theoretical kind. But besides helping us in the fundamental task of selecting problems, the technological approach imposes a discipline on our speculative inclinations (which, especially in the field of sociology proper, are liable to lead us into the region of metaphysics); for it forces us to submit our theories to definite standards, such as standards of clarity and practical testability. My point about the technological approach might perhaps be made by saying that sociology (and perhaps even the social sciences in general) should look, not indeed for 'its Newton or its Darwin',[3] but rather for its Galileo, or its Pasteur.

This and my previous references to an analogy between the methods of the social and the natural sciences are likely to provoke as much opposition as our choice of terms like 'social technology' and 'social engineering' (this in spite of the important qualification expressed by the word 'piecemeal'). So I had better say that I fully appreciate the importance of the fight against a dogmatic methodological naturalism or 'scientism' (to use Professor Hayek's term).

---

[3] See M. Ginsberg, in *Human Affairs* (ed. by R. B. Cattell and others [London: Macmillan & Co., 1937]), p. 180. It must be admitted, however, that the success of mathematical economics shows that one social science at least has gone through its Newtonian revolution.

Nevertheless I do not see why we should not make use of this analogy as far as it is fruitful, even though we recognize that it has been badly misused and misrepresented in certain quarters. Besides, we can hardly offer a stronger argument against these dogmatic naturalists than one that shows that some of the methods they attack are fundamentally the same as the methods used in the natural sciences.

A *prima facie* objection against what we call the technological approach is that it implies the adoption of an 'activist' attitude towards the social order . . . and that it is therefore liable to prejudice us against the anti-interventionist or 'passivist' view: the view that if we are dissatisfied with existing social or economic conditions, it is because we do not understand how they work and why active intervention could only make matters worse. Now I must admit that I am certainly out of sympathy with this 'passivist' view, and that I even believe that a policy of *universal* anti-interventionism is untenable—even on purely logical grounds, since its supporters are bound to recommend political intervention aimed at preventing intervention. Nevertheless, the technological approach as such is neutral in this matter (as indeed it ought to be), and by no means incompatible with anti-interventionism. On the contrary, I think that anti-interventionism involves a technological approach. For to assert that interventionism makes matters worse is to say that certain political actions would not have certain effects—to wit, not the desired ones; and it is one of the most characteristic tasks of any technology to *point out what cannot be achieved.*

It is worth while to consider this point more closely. As I have shown elsewhere,[4] every natural law can be expressed by asserting that *such and such a thing cannot happen;* that is to say, by a sentence in the form of the proverb: 'You can't carry water in a sieve.' For example, the law of conservation of energy can be expressed by: 'You cannot build a perpetual motion machine'; and that of entropy by: 'You cannot build a machine which is a hundred per cent efficient.' This way of formulating natural laws is one which makes their technological significance obvious and it may therefore be called the '*technological form*' of a natural law. If we now consider anti-interventionism in this light, then we see at once that it may well be expressed by sentences of the form: 'You cannot achieve such and such results', or perhaps, 'You cannot achieve

---

[4] See my *Logic of Scientific Discovery* (1959), section 15. (Negated existential propositions.) The theory may be contrasted with Mill, *Logic*, Book V, ch. V, section 2.

such and such ends without such and such concomitant effects.' But this shows that anti-interventionism can be called a typically *technological doctrine.*

It is not, of course, the only one in the realm of social science. On the contrary, the significance of our analysis lies in the fact that it draws attention to a really fundamental similarity between the natural and the social sciences. I have in mind the existence of sociological laws or hypotheses which are analogous to the laws or hypotheses of the natural sciences. Since the existence of such sociological laws or hypotheses (other than so-called 'historical laws') has often been doubted,[5] I will now give a number of examples: 'You cannot introduce agricultural tariffs and at the same time reduce the cost of living.'—'You cannot, in an industrial society, organize consumers' pressure groups as effectively as you can organize certain producers' pressure groups.'—'You cannot have a centrally planned society with a price system that fulfils the main functions of competitive prices.'—'You cannot have full employment without inflation.' Another group of examples may be taken from the realm of power politics: 'You cannot introduce a political reform without causing some repercussions which are undesirable from the point of view of the ends aimed at' (therefore, look out for them).—'You cannot introduce a political reform without strengthening the opposing forces, to a degree roughly in ratio to the scope of the reform.' (This may be said to be the technological corollary of 'There are always interests connected with the *status quo.*')—'You cannot make a revolution without causing a reaction.' To these examples we may add two more, which may be called 'Plato's law of revolutions' (from the eighth book of the *Republic*) and 'Lord Acton's law of corruption', respectively: 'You cannot make a successful revolution if the ruling class is not weakened by internal dissension or defeat in war.'—'You cannot give a man power over other men without tempting him to misuse it—a temptation which roughly increases with the amount of power wielded, and which very few are capable of resisting.' Nothing is here assumed about the strength of the available evidence in favour of these hypotheses whose formulations certainly leave much room for improvement. They are merely examples of the kind of statements

[5] See, for example, M. R. Cohen, *Reason and Nature* [New York: Harcourt, Brace & Co., 1931], pp. 356 ff. The examples in the text appear to refute this particular anti-naturalistic view.

which a piecemeal technology may attempt to discuss, and to substantiate.

## PIECEMEAL *versus* UTOPIAN ENGINEERING

Notwithstanding the objectionable associations which attach to the term 'engineering',[6] I shall use the term 'piecemeal social engineering' to describe the practical application of the results of piecemeal technology. The term is useful since there is need for a term covering social activities, private as well as public, which, in order to realize some aim or end, consciously utilize all available technological knowledge.[7] Piecemeal social engineering resembles physical engineering in regarding the *ends* as beyond the province of technology. (All that technology may say about ends is whether or not they are compatible with each other or realizable.) In this it differs from historicism, which regards the ends of human activities as dependent on historical forces and so within its province.

Just as the main task of the physical engineer is to design machines and to remodel and service them, the task of the piecemeal social engineer is to design social institutions, and to reconstruct and run those already in existence. The term 'social institution' is used here in a very wide sense, to include bodies of a private as well as of a public character. Thus I shall use it to describe a business, whether it is a small shop or an insurance company, and likewise a school, or an 'educational system', or a police force, or a Church, or a law court. The piecemeal technologist or engineer recognizes

[6] Against the use of the term 'social engineering' (in the 'piecemeal' sense) it has been objected by Professor Hayek that the typical engineering job involves the centralization of all relevant knowledge in a single head, whereas it is typical of all truly social problems that knowledge has to be used which cannot be so centralized. (See Hayek, *Collectivist Economic Planning* [London: Routledge & Kegan Paul Ltd.], 1935, p. 210.) I admit that this fact is of fundamental importance. It can be formulated by the technological hypothesis: 'You cannot centralize within a planning authority the knowledge relevant for such tasks as the satisfaction of personal needs, or the utilization of specialized skill and ability.' (A similar hypothesis may be proposed regarding the impossibility of centralizing initiative in connection with similar tasks.) The use of the term 'social engineering' may now be defended by pointing out that the engineer must use the technological knowledge embodied in these hypotheses which inform him of the limitations of his own initiative as well as of his own knowledge.

[7] Including, if it can be obtained, knowledge concerning the limitations of knowledge, as explained in the previous note.

that *only a minority of social institutions are consciously designed while the vast majority have just 'grown', as the undesigned results of human actions.*[8] But however strongly he may be impressed by this important fact, as a technologist or engineer he will look upon them from a 'functional' or 'instrumental' point of view.[9] He will see them as means to certain ends, or as convertible to the service of certain ends; as machines rather than as organisms. This does not mean, of course, that he will overlook the fundamental differences between institutions and physical instruments. On the contrary, the technologist should study the differences as well as the similarities, expressing his results in the form of hypotheses. And indeed, it is not difficult to formulate hypotheses about institutions in technological form as is shown by the following example: 'You cannot construct foolproof institutions, that is to say, institutions whose functioning does not very largely depend upon persons: institutions, at best, can reduce the uncertainty of the personal element, by assisting those who work for the aims for which the institutions are designed, and on whose personal initiative and knowledge success largely depends. (Institutions are like fortresses. They must be well designed *and* properly manned.)'[10]

The characteristic approach of the piecemeal engineer is this. Even though he may perhaps cherish some ideals which concern society 'as a whole'—its general welfare, perhaps—he does not believe in the method of re-designing it as a whole. Whatever his ends, he tries to achieve them by small adjustments and re-adjustments

[8] The two views—that social institutions are either 'designed' or that they just 'grow'—correspond to those of the Social Contract theorists and of their critics, for example, Hume. But Hume does not give up the 'functional' or 'instrumentalist' view of social institutions, for he says that men could not do without them. This position might be elaborated into a Darwinian explanation of the instrumental character of undesigned institutions (such as language): if they have no useful function, they have no chance of surviving. According to this view, undesigned social institutions may emerge as *unintended consequences of rational actions:* just as a road may be formed without any intention to do so by people who find it convenient to use a track already existing (as Descartes observes). It need hardly be stressed, however, that the technological approach is quite independent of all questions of 'origin'.

[9] For the 'functional' approach, see B. Malinowski, for example, 'Anthropology as the Basis of Social Science', in *Human Affairs* (ed. Cattell), especially pp. 206 ff. and 239 ff.

[10] This example, asserting that the efficiency of institutional 'machines' is limited, and that the functioning of institutions depends on their being supplied with proper personnel, may perhaps be compared with the principles of thermodynamics, such as the law of conservation of energy (in the form in

which can be continually improved upon. His ends may be of diverse kinds, for example, the accumulation of wealth or of power by certain individuals, or by certain groups; or the distribution of wealth and power; or the protection of certain 'rights' of individuals or groups, etc. Thus public or political social engineering may have the most diverse tendencies, totalitarian as well as liberal. (Examples of far-reaching liberal programmes for piecemeal reform have been given by W. Lippmann, under the title 'The Agenda of Liberalism'.[11]) The piecemeal engineer knows, like Socrates, how little he knows. He knows that we can learn only from our mistakes. Accordingly, he will make his way, step by step, carefully comparing the results expected with the results achieved, and always on the look-out for the unavoidable unwanted consequences of any reform; and he will avoid undertaking reforms of a complexity and scope which make it impossible for him to disentangle causes and effects, and to know what he is really doing.

Such 'piecemeal tinkering' does not agree with the political temperament of many 'activists'. Their programme, which too has been described as a programme of 'social engineering', may be called 'holistic' or 'Utopian engineering'.

Holistic or Utopian social engineering, as opposed to piecemeal social engineering, is never of a 'private' but always of a 'public' character. It aims at remodelling the 'whole of society' in accordance with a definite plan or blueprint; it aims at 'seizing the key positions'[12] and at extending 'the power of the State . . . until the State becomes nearly identical with society',[13] and it aims, further-

---

which it excludes the possibility of a perpetual motion machine). As such, it may be contrasted with other 'scientistic' attempts to work out an analogy between the physical concept of energy and some sociological concepts such as power; see, for example, Bertrand Russell's *Power* ([London: George Allen & Unwin, Ltd.], 1938), p. 10 f., where this kind of scientistic attempt is made. I do not think that Russell's main point—that the various 'forms of power', such as wealth, propagandist power, naked power, may sometimes be 'converted' into one another—can be expressed in technological form.

[11] W. Lippmann, *The Good Society* ([Boston: Little, Brown & Co.], 1937), ch. XI, pp. 203 ff. See also W. H. Hutt, *Plan for Reconstruction* ([London: Routledge & Kegan Paul Ltd.], 1943).

[12] The expression is often used by K. Mannheim in his *Man and Society in an Age of Reconstruction* [London: Routledge & Kegan Paul Ltd., 1940]; see his Index, and, for example, pp. 269, 295, 320, 381. This book is the most elaborate exposition of a holistic and historicist programme known to me and is therefore singled out here for criticism.

[13] See Mannheim, *ibid.*, 337.

more, at controlling from these 'key positions' the historical forces that mould the future of the developing society: either by arresting this development, or else by foreseeing its course and adjusting society to it.

It may be questioned, perhaps, whether the piecemeal and holistic approaches here described are fundamentally different, considering that we have put no limits to the scope of a piecemeal approach. As this approach is understood here, constitutional reform, for example, falls well within its scope; nor shall I exclude the possibility that a series of piecemeal reforms might be inspired by one general tendency, for example, a tendency towards a greater equalization of incomes. In this way, piecemeal methods may lead to changes in what is usually called the 'class structure of society'. Is there any difference, it may be asked, between these more ambitious kinds of piecemeal engineering and the holistic or Utopian approach? And this question may become even more pertinent if we consider that, when trying to assess the likely consequences of some proposed reform, the piecemeal technologist must do his best to estimate the effects of any measure upon the 'whole' of society.

In answering this question, I shall not attempt to draw a precise line of demarcation between the two methods, but I shall try to bring out the very different point of view from which the holist and the piecemeal technologist look upon the task of reforming society. The holists reject the piecemeal approach as being too modest. Their rejection of it, however, does not quite square with their practice; for in practice they always fall back on a somewhat haphazard and clumsy although ambitious and ruthless application of what is essentially a piecemeal method without its cautious and self-critical character. The reason is that, in practice, the holistic method turns out to be impossible; the greater the holistic changes attempted, the greater are their unintended and largely unexpected repercussions, forcing upon the holistic engineer the expedient of piecemeal *improvization*. In fact, this expedient is more characteristic of centralized or collectivistic planning than of the more modest and careful piecemeal intervention; and it continually leads the Utopian engineer to do things which he did not intend to do; that is to say, it leads to the notorious phenomenon of *unplanned planning*. Thus the difference between Utopian and piecemeal engineering turns out, in practice, to be a difference not so much in scale and scope as in caution and in preparedness for unavoidable surprises. One could also say that, in practice, the two *methods* differ in other ways than in scale and scope—in opposition to what we are led to expect if we compare the two *doctrines* concerning the proper methods of rational social reform. Of these two doctrines, I hold that the one is true, while the other is false and liable to lead to mistakes which are both avoidable and grave. Of the two methods, I hold that one is possible, while the other simply does not exist: it is impossible.

One of the differences between the Utopian or holistic approach and the piecemeal approach may therefore be stated in this way: while the piecemeal engineer can attack his problem with an open mind as to the scope of the reform, the holist cannot do this; for he has decided beforehand that a complete reconstruction is possible and necessary. This fact has far-reaching consequences. It prejudices the Utopianist against certain sociological hypotheses which state limits to institutional control; for example, the one mentioned above in this section, expressing the uncertainty due to the personal element, the 'human factor'. By a rejection *a priori* of such hypotheses, the Utopian approach violates the principles of scientific method. On the other hand, problems connected with the uncertainty of the human factor must force the Utopianist, whether he likes it or not, to try to control the human factor by institutional means, and to extend his programme so as to embrace not only the transformation of society, according to plan, but also the transformation of man.[14] 'The political problem, therefore, is to *organize human impulses* in such a way that they will direct their energy to the right strategic points, and steer the total process of development in the desired direction.' It seems to escape the well-meaning Utopianist that this programme implies an admission of failure, even before he launches it. For it substitutes for his demand that we build a new society, fit for men and women to live in, the demand that we 'mould' these men and women to fit into his new society. This, clearly, removes any possibility of testing the success or failure of the new society. For those who do not like living in it only admit thereby that they are not yet fit to live in it; that their 'human impulses' need further 'organizing'. But without the possibility of tests, any claim that a 'scientific' method is being employed evaporates. The holistic approach is incompatible with a truly scientific attitude.

[14] 'The Problem of Transforming Man' is the heading of a chapter of Mannheim's *Man and Society*. The following quotation is from that chapter, p. 199 f.

JOSEPH A. SCHUMPETER

# Is the History of Economics
# a History of Ideologies?

*Popper opposes piecemeal social engineering to the wholesale "Utopian"*
*projects of reform which he would ascribe to Marxist revolutionaries*
*(among others). Marxists, hotly controverting his approach, would de-*
*nounce it as inspired by protective bourgeois ideology. The charge of*
*ideology, as Schumpeter acknowledges, reaches farther than the difficulty*
*(which social scientists have much discussed) of personal bias or preju-*
*dice. Ideology imposes limits, invisible to the participants, on the process*
*of social interaction—the exchange of criticisms—which scientists mainly*
*rely on to expose bias. The answer to the charge is appropriately under-*
*taken with specific reference to economics, because economics—the*
*"classical" liberal economics of laissez-faire—was Marx's chief target; and*
*on the world scene his accusations are still alive.*

*Joseph A. Schumpeter (1883–1950) was educated in Austria and taught*
*there until after the First World War. Austrian Minister of Finance (1919–*
*1920), professor of economics at Bonn (1925–1932), and professor at*
*Harvard from 1932 to his death, he remains famous for his theories about*
*economic development under capitalism, his treatment of business cycles,*
*and the great history of ideas from which the following selection is taken.*

[(a) *Special Nature of 'Economic Laws.'*] The historical or 'evolutionary' nature of the economic process unquestionably limits the
scope of general concepts and of general relations between them
('economic laws') that economists may be able to formulate. There
is indeed no sense in denying, a priori, as has been done sometimes,
that any such concepts or relations can be formulated at all. In
particular it is not necessary that the concepts we use in the study
of social groups should be familiar to the members of these groups
themselves: the fact, if it be a fact, that the concept of income was
not familiar to the people of the Middle Ages before the fourteenth

century is no reason for not using it in an analysis of their economy.[1] But it is true that 'economic laws' are much less stable than are the 'laws' of any physical science, that they work out differently in different institutional conditions, and that neglect of this fact has been responsible for many an aberration. It is also true that whenever we attempt to interpret human attitudes, especially attitudes of people far removed from us in time or culture, we risk misunderstanding them not only if we crudely substitute our own attitudes for theirs, but also if we do our best to penetrate into the working of their minds. All this is made much worse than it would be otherwise by the fact that the analyzing observer himself is the product of a given social environment—and of his particular location in this environment—that conditions him to see certain things rather than others, and to see them in a certain light. And even this is not all: environmental factors may even endow the observer with a subconscious craving to see things in a certain light. This brings us up to the problem of ideological bias in economic analysis.

Modern psychology and psychotherapy have made us familiar with a habit of our minds that we call rationalization. This habit consists in comforting ourselves and impressing others by drawing a picture of ourselves, our motives, our friends, our enemies, our vocation, our church, our country, which may have more to do with what we like them to be than with what they are. The competitor who is more successful than we are ourselves is likely to owe his success to tricks that we despise. As likely as not, the leader of a party not our own is a charlatan. The beloved girl is an angel exempt from human frailties. The enemy country is the home of monsters, our own the home of wholly admirable heroes. And so on. The importance of this habit for the health and happiness of the normal

---

[1] Let me make this quite clear. Sociologists like Max Weber who stand for the interpretative method of social states or changes—that is, who believe that it is our main or sole business to try to understand what things meant to the people concerned—may easily drift into the position that the use of any concepts not familiar to the people under study involves the error of assuming that their minds functioned just like ours. Now this error may be involved but it need not be: using a concept that carries meaning for us but not to the people that we observe is one thing; postulating that the concept carried meaning also for the latter is another thing. We need not go to primitive tribes in order to illustrate this: if, in terms of concepts of our own, we formulate the conditions for maximizing profits, we need not assume that the businessman himself uses these concepts; our 'theory' is perfectly meaningful even if we know that he does not.

mind is obvious and so is the importance of a correct diagnosis of its verbal manifestations.

[(b) *The Marxian Exposition of Ideological Bias.*] Half a century before the full importance of this phenomenon was professionally recognized and put to use, Marx and Engels discovered it and used their discovery in their criticisms of the 'bourgeois' economics of their time. Marx realized that men's ideas or systems of ideas are not, as historiography is still prone to assume uncritically, the prime movers of the historical process, but form a 'superstructure' on more fundamental factors, as will be explained at the proper place in our narrative. Marx realized further that the ideas or systems of ideas that prevail at any given time in any given social group are, so far as they contain propositions about facts and inferences from facts, likely to be vitiated for exactly the same reasons that also vitiate a man's theories about his own individual behavior. That is to say, people's ideas are likely to glorify the interests and actions of the classes that are in a position to assert themselves and therefore are likely to draw or to imply pictures of them that may be seriously at variance with the truth. Thus, the medieval knights fancied themselves as protectors of the weak and defenders of the Christian faith, whereas their actual behavior and, still more, other factors that had produced and kept in existence the social structure of their world are bound to look very different to an observer of a different time and class. Such systems of ideas Marx called ideologies.[2] And his contention was that a large part of the economics of his time was nothing but the ideology of the industrial and commercial bourgeoisie. The value of this great contribution to our insight into the processes of history and into the meaning of social science is impaired but not destroyed by three blemishes, which it is as well to notice at once.

First, while Marx was so much alive to the ideological character of systems of ideas with which he was not in sympathy, he was completely blind to the ideological elements present in his own. But the principle of interpretation involved in his concept of ide-

[2] The term is of French origin and at first meant simply the analysis of ideas, especially with reference to Condillac's theory. Occasionally it seems to have been used in much the same sense as the term Moral Philosophy, i.e. as roughly equivalent to social science. In this sense it was used by Destutt de Tracy. Napoleon I also used it but in a different sense that carried a derogatory connotation: he described as *idéologues* those opponents of his government, such as Lafayette, whom he considered unrealistic dreamers.

ology is perfectly general. Obviously we cannot say: everywhere else is ideology; we alone stand on the rock of absolute truth. Laborist ideologies are neither better nor worse than are any others.

Second, the Marxist analysis of ideological systems of thought reduces them to emulsions of class interests which are in turn defined in exclusively economic terms. According to Marx the ideologies of capitalist society are, to put it crudely, glorifications of the interests of what he styled the capitalist class, whose interests are made to turn on the hunt for pecuniary profits. Ideologies that do not glorify the behavior of capitalist man in business but something else, for instance the national character and behavior, must hence always be reducible, however indirectly, to those economic interests of the dominant class. This however is not implied in the principle of ideological interpretation but constitutes an additional and much more doubtful theory. The principle itself implies only two things: that ideologies are superstructures erected on, and produced by, the realities of the objective social structure below them; and that they tend to reflect these realities in a characteristically biased manner. Whether or not these realities can be completely described in purely economic terms is another question. Without entering upon it here, we merely record the fact that we are going to attach a much wider meaning to the concept of Ideological Influence. Social location undoubtedly is a powerful factor in shaping our *minds*. But this does not amount to saying that our minds are exclusively shaped by the economic elements in our class position or that, even so far as this is the case, they are exclusively shaped by a well-defined class or group *interest*.

Third, Marx and especially the majority of his followers assumed too readily that statements which display ideological influence are ipso facto condemned thereby. But it cannot be emphasized too strongly that, like individual rationalizations, ideologies are not lies. It must be added that statements of fact that enter into them are not necessarily erroneous. The temptation is great to avail oneself of the opportunity to dispose at one stroke of a whole body of propositions one does not like, by the simple device of calling it an ideology. This device is no doubt very effective, as effective as are attacks upon an opponent's personal motives. But logically it is inadmissible. As pointed out already, explanation, however correct, of the reasons why a man says what he says tells us nothing about whether it is true or false. Similarly statements that proceed from an ideological background are open to suspicion, but they may still be perfectly valid. Both Galileo and his opponents may have been swayed by ideologies. That does not prevent us from saying that he was 'right.' But what logical warrant have we for saying so? Is there any means of locating, recognizing, and possibly eliminating the ideologically vitiated elements in economic analysis? And does enough remain when we have done so? . . .

. . . Ideological bias, as defined above by our amended version of the Marxist definition, is obviously not the only danger that threatens economic analysis. In particular there are two others that should be mentioned specifically because they are easily confused with ideological bias. One is possible tampering with facts or with rules of procedure by Special Pleaders. All we have to say about this has been said already: here I only wish to warn the reader that special pleading is not the same thing as ideologically vitiated analyzing. Another danger proceeds from the inveterate habit of economists to pass value judgments upon the processes they observe. An economist's value judgments often *reveal* his ideology but they *are not* his ideology: it is possible to pass value judgments upon irreproachably established facts and the relations between them, and it is possible to refrain from passing any value judgments upon facts that are seen in an ideologically deflected light.[3] . . .

[(c) *How Does a History of Economic Analysis Differ from a History of Systems of Political Economy; from a History of Economic Thought?*] The distinction above between ideologically biased statements and value judgments should not, however, be interpreted as a denial of their affinity. This affinity is even the main reason why I think it important to distinguish this history of economics—economic analysis—from either a history of Systems of Political Economy or a history of Economic Thought. By a system of political economy I mean an exposition of a comprehensive set of economic policies that its author advocates on the strength of certain unifying (normative) principles such as the principles of

---

[3] Some groups, like bureaucracies, are . . . given to . . . the clearly ideological denial of any group interest of their own or at least of its influence on the policies that they originate or assist in shaping. This may be used as a first example of the influence of ideologies upon analysis. For this ideology of bureaucracies is an important factor in the unscientific habit of economists of using a clearly ideological theory of the state that raises the latter into a superhuman agency for the public good and neglects all the facts about the realities of public administration that modern political science provides.

economic liberalism, of socialism, and so on. Such systems do come within our range so far as they contain genuinely analytic work. For instance, A. Smith's *Wealth of Nations* was, in fact as in intention, a system of political economy in the sense just defined and as such it does not interest us. All the more does it interest us by virtue of the fact that A. Smith's political principles and recipes— his guarded advocacy of free trade and the rest—are but the cloak of a great analytic achievement. In other words, we are not so much interested in *what* he argued for as we are in *how* he argued and what tools of analysis he used in doing so. His political principles and recipes themselves (including ideology—revealing value judgments) were no doubt what mattered most to himself and to his readers and, furthermore, what accounts primarily for the success of his work with the public and, in this sense, for its proud position in the history of human thought. But I am prepared to surrender them all as mere formulations of the ideology of his epoch and country, without validity for any other.

The same applies to what we define as Economic Thought, that is, the sum total of all the opinions and desires concerning economic subjects, especially concerning public policy bearing upon these subjects that, at any given time and place, float in the public mind. Now the public mind is never an undifferentiated or homogeneous something but is the result of the division of the corresponding community into groups and classes of various natures. In other words, the public mind reflects more or less treacherously, and at some times more treacherously than at others, the class structure of the corresponding society and the group minds or attitudes that form in it. Since these group minds have different opportunities of asserting themselves and especially of leaving their marks upon the literature which comes under the observation of later generations, questions of interpretation arise that are always difficult and sometimes impossible to solve. The public mind of a time and place is in particular not only differentiated sectionally, but also according to the position and intelligence of the individuals that form the same horizontal or vertical section. It is one thing with politicians, another with the shopkeepers, farmers, and laborers that are 'represented' by these politicians. And it may be formulated into systems of political economy by writers who belong, or who attach themselves, to particular sections. On the other hand, it may border on, or overlap with, analytic work as it has often done in treatises written by members of the commercial or industrial bourgeoisie. So far as it does do the latter, it will of course be our task to pick out as best we can such analytic performances from the common run of verbalizations of the humors of the times that are unconnected with any effort to improve our conceptual apparatus, and hence without interest for us. However difficult it may be to carry out this program in any particular case, the distinction between different masses of thought which we are trying to draw is quite clear on principle. . . .

The development of analytic work, however much disturbed it may have been by the interests and attitudes of the market place, displays a characteristic property which is completely absent from the historical development of economic thought in our sense and also from the historical succession of systems of political economy. This property may best be illustrated by an example: from the earliest times until today, analytic economists have been interested, more or less, in the analysis of the phenomenon that we call competitive price. When the modern student meets the phenomenon on an advanced level of his study, for instance in the books of Hicks or Samuelson,[4] he is introduced to a number of concepts and problems that may seem to him difficult at first, and would certainly have been completely un-understandable to so relatively recent an author as John Stuart Mill. But the student will also discover before long that a new apparatus poses and solves problems for which the older authors could hardly have found answers even if they had been aware of them. This defines in a common-sense and at any rate a perfectly unambiguous manner, in what sense there has been 'scientific progress' between Mill and Samuelson. It is the same sense in which we may say that there has been technological progress in the extraction of teeth between the times of John Stuart Mill and our own.

Now our ability to speak of progress in these cases is obviously due to the fact that there is a widely accepted standard, confined, of course, to a group of professionals, that enables us to array different theories of competitive price in a series, each member of which can be unambiguously labeled superior to the preceding one. We further observe that this array is associated with the lapse of

[4] J. R. Hicks, English economist (1904–    ); Paul A. Samuelson, American economist (1915–    ). Their most famous theoretical works are Hicks' *Value and Capital* (Oxford: Clarendon Press, 2d ed., 1946) and Samuelson's *Foundations of Economic Analysis* (Cambridge: Harvard University Press, 1947)—not to be confused with his widely used introductory textbook.—Ed.

time, in the sense that the later theory of competitive price almost always holds higher rank in the array of analytic perfection: whenever this is not the case, it is possible to assign this fact to extra-analytic and, in this sense, disturbing influences. But while it is thus possible to speak of analytic progress and impossible to deny the facts that this word is to denote, there is nothing corresponding to this in the field of economic thought or even in any historical array of systems of political economy. For instance, there would be no sense in speaking of a superiority of Charlemagne's ideas on economic policy as revealed by his legislative and administrative actions over the economic ideas of, say, King Hammurabi; or of the general principles of policy revealed by the proclamations of the Stuart kings over those of Charlemagne; or of the declarations of policy that sometimes preface acts of Congress over those Stuart proclamations. . . .

[(d) *The Scientific Process: Vision and Rules of Procedure.*] We are now ready to take the second step in our inquiry into the dangers of ideological bias, namely, to ask the question how far it threatens the validity of results in that narrower field that we have described as Economic Analysis. Some readers may think even that there is no second step to take: since we have already surrendered, as ideologically conditioned, all the systems of political economy, and since, in addition, we have recognized as ideologies the less completely systematized sets of opinions on economic subjects that, at any time and place, 'float in the public mind,' we seem in fact to have admitted all there is to admit. And those readers in particular whose primary interest is in the history of the ideas that shape or, at all events, are closely associated with policies or with people's ideas about what is to be considered as fair or desirable in the management of economic affairs and whose interest in the development of technical economic analysis is secondary only are quite likely to grant—perhaps with a shrug of the shoulders—that our box of tools may well be as far removed from the influence of ideologies as are the techniques of any other science. Unfortunately we cannot take this for granted. Let us therefore analyze the scientific process itself in order to see where ideological elements may enter it and what are our means of recognizing and perhaps eliminating them.

In practice we all start our own research from the work of our predecessors, that is, we hardly ever start from scratch. But suppose we did start from scratch, what are the steps we should have to take? Obviously, in order to be able to posit to ourselves any problems at all, we should first have to visualize a distinct set of coherent phenomena as a worth-while object of our analytic efforts. In other words, analytic effort is of necessity preceded by a pre-analytic cognitive act that supplies the raw material for the analytic effort. In this book, this preanalytic cognitive act will be called Vision. It is interesting to note that vision of this kind not only must precede historically the emergence of analytic effort in any field but also may re-enter the history of every established science each time somebody teaches us to *see* things in a light of which the source is not to be found in the facts, methods, and results of the pre-existing state of the science.

Let us illustrate this at once by an outstanding example from our own field and time. Critics and admirers of the scientific performance of the late Lord Keynes will agree to the statement that his *General Theory of Employment, Interest, and Money* (1936) was the outstanding success of the 1930's and that it dominated analytic work for a decade after its publication, to say the least. The *General Theory* presented an analytic apparatus which the author summed up in Chapter 18. If we follow his exposition step by step (see especially pp. 249–54) we observe that this apparatus had been designed in order to give convenient expression to certain facts of 'the world in which we live'—although, as Keynes himself emphasized, these facts are attributed to his fundamental schedules (propensity to consume, attitude to liquidity, and marginal efficiency of capital) [5] as special characteristics and not as 'logically necessary' properties. This analytic pattern will be discussed in the proper place,[6] where it will also be shown that the special characteristics in question are the characteristics of England's aging capitalism as seen from the standpoint of an English intellectual. There can be no question of their having been established by antecedent factual

[5] These are all concepts used by Keynes to explain how total investment originates in decisions by firms or persons: personal decisions—related by a given historical schedule or function to variations in income—to spend on current consumption or hold back from consumption; personal and corporate decisions to hold liquid assets (money) or invest in capital goods. Less profitable investments—where the marginal efficiency or (expected) return on capital is lower—will be made only when lower rates of interest prevail; but at lower rates of interest the liquidity-preference schedule or function may be such that the demand for liquid assets would exceed the quantity of money available.—Ed.

[6] See Part v, ch. 5 of the *History of Economic Analysis*.

research. They are 'plausibly ascribed to our [the English] world, on our general knowledge of contemporary human nature' (p. 250). This is not the place to discuss the merits or demerits of this conception. All that matters here and now is that it *is* a conception or vision in our sense, and that it antedated all the analytic efforts that Keynes and others bestowed upon it. The process stands out in this case with such unsurpassable clearness because we can read a formulation of the vision, as yet analytically unarmed, in a few brilliant pages of Keynes's *The Economic Consequences of the Peace* (1919). So far as this line of endeavor of a man of many interests was concerned, the whole period between 1919 and 1936 was then spent in attempts, first unsuccessful, then increasingly successful, at implementing the particular vision of the economic process of our time that was fixed in Keynes's mind by 1919 at latest. Other examples, from our field as well as from others, could be adduced in order to illustrate this 'way of our mind.' But it would hardly be possible to find a more telling one.

Analytic effort starts when we have conceived our vision of the set of phenomena that caught our interest, no matter whether this set lies in virgin soil or in land that had been cultivated before. The first task is to verbalize the vision or to conceptualize it in such a way that its elements take their places, with names attached to them that facilitate recognition and manipulation, in a more or less orderly schema or picture. But in doing so we almost automatically perform two other tasks. On the one hand, we assemble further facts in addition to those perceived already, and learn to distrust others that figured in the original vision; on the other hand, the very work of constructing the schema or picture will add further relations and concepts to, and in general also eliminate others from, the original stock. Factual work and 'theoretical' work, in an endless relation of give and take, naturally testing one another and setting new tasks for each other, will eventually produce *scientific models*, the provisional joint products of their interaction with the surviving elements of the original vision, to which increasingly more rigorous standards of consistency and adequacy will be applied. This is indeed a primitive but not, I think, misleading statement of the process by which we grind out what we call scientific propositions. Now it should be perfectly clear that there is a wide gate for ideology to enter into this process. In fact, it enters on the very ground floor, into the preanalytic cognitive act of which we have been speaking. Analytic work begins with material provided by our vision of things, and this vision is ideological almost by definition. It embodies the picture of things as we see them, and wherever there is any possible motive for wishing to see them in a given rather than another light, the way in which we see things can hardly be distinguished from the way in which we wish to see them. The more honest and naïve our vision is, the more dangerous is it to the eventual emergence of anything for which general validity can be claimed. The inference for the social sciences is obvious, and it is not even true that he who hates a social system will form an objectively more correct vision of it than he who loves it. For love distorts indeed, but hate distorts still more. Our only comfort is in the fact that there is a large number of phenomena that fail to affect our emotions one way or the other, and that therefore look to one man very much as they do to another. But we also observe that the rules of procedure that we apply in our analytic work are almost as much exempt from ideological influence as vision is subject to it. Passionate allegiance and passionate hatred may indeed tamper with these rules. In themselves these rules, many of which, moreover, are imposed upon us by the scientific practice in fields that are little or not at all affected by ideology, are pretty effective in showing up misuse. And, what is equally important, they tend to crush out ideologically conditioned error from the visions from which we start. It is their particular virtue, and they do so automatically and irrespective of the desires of the research worker. The new facts he is bound to accumulate impose themselves upon his schema. The new concepts and relations, which somebody else will formulate if he does not, must verify his ideologies or else destroy them. And if this process is allowed to work itself out completely, it will indeed not protect us from the emergence of new ideologies, but it will clear in the end the existing ones from error. It is true that in economics, and still more in other social sciences, this sphere of the strictly provable is limited in that there are always fringe ends of things that are matters of personal experience and impression from which it is practically impossible to drive ideology, or for that matter conscious dishonesty, completely. The comfort we may take from our argument is therefore never complete. But it does cover most of the ground in the sense of narrowing the sphere of ideologically vitiated propositions considerably, that is, of narrowing it down and of making it always possible to locate the spots in which it may be active.

# Bibliography

## SUGGESTIONS FOR FURTHER READING

1. Comprehensive treatments of the philosophical problems of the social sciences can be found in a number of works, among them Robert Brown, *Explanation in Social Science* (London: Routledge, 1963); and Quentin Gibson, *The Logic of Social Enquiry* (London: Routledge, 1960). Brown stresses problems close to the preoccupations of social scientists; Gibson is more inclined to stress problems that preoccupy philosophers. Before doing any further reading in general methodology, however, the beginning student would do well to establish a concrete feeling for the statistical aspects of social research by reading W. Allen Wallis and Harry V. Roberts' lively paperback, *The Nature of Statistics* (New York: Collier Books, 1962); and he is unlikely to find other comprehensive treatments that excel Chaps. 13 and 14 of Ernest Nagel's *The Structure of Science* (New York: Harcourt, 1961) in succinctness and solidity. Maurice Natanson's anthology, *Philosophy of the Social Sciences* (New York: Random, 1963) contains a number of interesting essays, including a lucid discussion of "ideal types" by Carl G. Hempel.

2. In *The Social System* (Glencoe, Ill.: The Free Press, 1951), Talcott Parsons draws a distinction (pp. 541–545) between "behavior" and "action" that roughly resembles the one at issue in the present book, but applies it with a heavy and restrictive hand to Skinner's behaviorism. The range of Skinner's claims and of his arguments for them is best appreciated by reading the whole of his *Science and Human Behavior* (New York: Macmillan, 1953).

3. Recent philosophical studies of "action" include Stuart Hampshire, *Thought and Action* (London: Chatto, 1959); and A. I. Melden, *Free Action* (London: Routledge, 1961). See also Melden's essay, "Action," in *The Philosophical Review*, October 1956, pp. 523–541. Some discussions of historical explanation stress the same topic, for instance, Chap. 5 ("The Rationale of Actions") of William Dray's *Laws and Explanation in History* (London: Oxford Univ. Press, 1957).

4. Current philosophical interest in the concept of rules and in the connection of rules with language and action reflects the influence of Ludwig Wittgenstein: see his *Philosophical Investigations* (Oxford: Blackwell, 1953). His ideas are drawn upon by Peter Winch in *The Idea of a Social Science* (London: Routledge, 1958) to support the extravagant thesis that the tasks of philosophy swallow up those of social science, both being concerned with explicating the rules of social action. (Reflection on Winch's book largely determined, in assent and dissent, the shape and contents of

the present one.) For further light on the subject of rules, the student might consult John Rawls' article, "Two Concepts of Rules," in *The Philosophical Review,* January 1955, pp. 3–32; Max Black, "The Analysis of Rules," in his *Models and Metaphors* (Ithaca: Cornell Univ. Press, 1962), a collection which also contains an interesting essay on "Models and Archetypes"; and Georg H. von Wright, *Norm and Action* (London: Routledge, 1963). See also the essay by Moore and Anderson referred to in the Introduction to the present book, p. 10 above; and, for a cautionary view, the appendix on rules and language to Chap. 1 of Paul Ziff's *Semantic Analysis* (Ithaca: Cornell Univ. Press, 1960).

   5. To appreciate the importance attributed to rules by social scientists, compare E. E. Evans-Pritchard, *Social Anthropology* (London: Cohen, 1951), especially pp. 19–20, with Clyde Kluckhohn, *Mirror for Man* (New York: McGraw, 1949), especially Chap. 2. The usage of "norm" in social scientists' writings is very complex and often (though related) does not directly parallel the usage of "rule." Writers like George C. Homans, in *Social Behavior: Its Elementary Forms* (New York: Harcourt, 1961), Chap. 6, and Robin M. Williams, Jr., *American Society* (2d ed.; New York: Knopf, 1963), p. 24, do, however, insist upon the parallel. Among social scientists, the profoundest writer on rules was perhaps Emile Durkheim (1858–1917). The relevant passages on "anomie" (i.e., "rulelessness") and solidarity from his works on suicide and the division of labor are most easily accessible in C. Wright Mills (ed.), *Images of Man* (New York: Braziller, 1960), pp. 449–485.